The NORTHERN LIGHT WITHIN

BLOOM IN WINTER
SHINE IN EVERY SEASON

ASHISH SINGH

The Northern Light Within: Bloom in Winter Shine in Every Season

For permissions, contact:
The Calm Mind Solutions Inc.
Toronto, Canada
✉ *connect@thecalmmind.co*
🌐 *www.thecalmmind.co*

Disclaimer

This book is intended for educational, informational, and personal development purposes only. It reflects the author's personal experiences, reflections, and practices that have supported well-being for himself and his clients.

It is not a substitute for professional medical, psychological, or therapeutic advice, diagnosis, or treatment. Readers are encouraged to use discretion and consult qualified healthcare professionals before undertaking any new breathing, meditation, or lifestyle practice—particularly if they have pre-existing health conditions, are pregnant, or are under medical supervision.

Every effort has been made to ensure the accuracy of the information presented. However, the author and publisher make no warranties or guarantees, express or implied, and disclaim any liability for loss, injury, or adverse outcomes arising directly or indirectly from the use or application of the material contained herein.

By reading this book, you agree to take full responsibility for your own health, safety, and well-being. Approach each practice gently, with self-awareness and care.

The reflections and techniques described draw inspiration from traditional mindfulness, yoga, and breathwork principles that exist within the public domain and ancient wisdom traditions. Their descriptions, sequencing, and interpretations are original to the author.

Metaphors such as the North Star and the Northern Light Within are used as symbolic representations of inner guidance and alignment, not as religious, scientific, or therapeutic claims.

Trademarks

Publishing Information

First Edition — 2025
Published in Canada / Distributed Worldwide
ISBN: 978-1-0698609-0-3

Library and Cataloguing
A CIP (Cataloguing-in-Publication) record may be available from Library and Archives Canada.

The Northern Light Within

Bloom in Winter Shine in Every Season

This book moves in three parts. By the end, you'll discover a set of gentle, evidence-informed practices designed to help you navigate any winter in your life—outer or inner—with greater clarity, resilience, and joy.

A Note before you begin vii

Prelude – The Northern Light Within – An Invitation to the Season Ahead xiii

PART I – THE WINTER LOOP 1

Foundational practices that build step by step:

1. Acceptance: The First Lens of Winter 3
2. Openness: The Second Breath of Winter 23
3. Nourishment: Feeding Body, Mind, and Spirit 37
4. Breathe and Believe: Breath, Meditation, and Visualization as Anchors 59
5. Words We Are Breathing: Affirmations as Inner Climate 93
6. Winter Gratitude: Widening Perspective 111
7. From Inner Critic to Inner Coach: Completing the Loop with Kindness 127

PART II – READY COMPANIONS 149

Practical supports for when life or work throws you off track:

8. The Loneliness: Growing Your Light & Pruning What Drains It 151

9. The Happy List: Your Personal Winter Medicine Cabinet — Small Joys and Resilience Boosters 165

10. Carrying Your Calm: Bringing Inner Practices to Work and Beyond 183

PART III – RETURNING & CARRYING FORWARD 199

Sustaining your progress and moving into brighter seasons:

11. When Old Leaves Return: Watchouts for Relapse and Self-Sabotage 201

12. Bloom in Winter – Shine in every Season: Carrying These Practices Forward 211

Epilogue 223

About the Author 225

Notes & Sources 227

Acknowledgments

To my wife, Gunjan, and to my parents — without your unwavering support, patience, and belief, this book would never have come into being. You held the space for me to write, to reflect, and to grow. Every page carries a piece of your love, and for that I am endlessly grateful.

A Note Before You Begin

This book isn't a checklist. It's a companion you can actually live with. Think of it as a seven-course meal served slowly, not a buffet you're expected to clear. Because there's no one-size-fits-all, you'll find multiple practices that have worked for me and my clients. You're not meant to do everything at once.

Your First Responsibility Is to Yourself

Most of us wear many hats — parent, partner, leader, caregiver, teammate, friend. We pour energy into each role until our own well runs dry. But tending to your inner steadiness is not indulgence; it is maintenance. It is a sacred responsibility that allows every other role to flourish. When you are calmer, you think more clearly; when you are nourished, you show up more generously.

This book is about that inner maintenance — the steady tending of your own light so that every hat you wear fits better. It will not ask you to overhaul your life. It will help you build small, portable practices that fit inside it.

Your Companion Guide: Using This Book Day-to-Day

Rather than "instructions," think of this as your pocket guide for weaving the practices into real life.

- One at a time: Start with one practice from each of the first seven chapters. Together they form a loop — a rhythm of support for winter's challenges. Add as you go, layer by layer.
- Ready companions: Chapters 8–12 are quick guides you can return to when life or work throw you off track.
- Tiny time windows: Even 5–15 minutes a day of deliberate practice can begin to shift how your mind and body respond to stress and build resilience over time.

Depth comes from consistency, not quantity. Think of this as a "Choose-Your-Own Winter Companion" rather than a curriculum.

But here's the most important part: this book is not about waiting. Not waiting for the season to change, the sky to brighten, or the perfect moment to arrive. Too often we postpone joy — "After winter, I'll feel better. After this project… after I heal." Postponing joy is how years slip by.

The truth is simpler — and harder: peace cannot be scheduled. Happiness does not begin in spring. It begins where you are — this breath, this season, this room. Winter is the lens here because winter strips life down to essentials. But the practices inside — acceptance, nourishment, breath, affirmations, gratitude, kindness, workplace rituals, community, and more — are not seasonal. They are seeds. What you plant now will grow through any storm, any season, any setback.

You'll notice short reflection prompts scattered throughout these pages — gentle invitations to pause, breathe, or write. Some appear at the end of a chapter; others meet you in the middle of a story or practice. You can simply reflect on them in the moment, or jot your thoughts in a journal, notebook, or whatever space feels natural.

What matters is not where you record them, but that you do — because pausing to reflect helps the insight shift from something read to something lived. These prompts are small anchors of awareness — pauses designed to bring the words off the page and into your life.

A Gentle Note on Safety

The practices and breathing techniques in this book are intended to support awareness, calm, and self-connection. They are not a substitute for professional medical or psychological care.

If you have any health conditions — particularly those affecting your lungs, heart, blood pressure, or anxiety — or if you are pregnant or under medical supervision, please consult a qualified healthcare provider before beginning any practice.

If at any point you feel lightheaded, short of breath, or uncomfortable, stop immediately and return to your natural breath. Proceed gently; your well-being always comes first. The author and publisher disclaim any liability for injury, loss, or adverse outcome resulting from the use or application of the information in this book. Readers are solely responsible for their own physical, mental, and emotional well-being in applying any of the techniques described. Engage with these practices mindfully and at your own discretion.

Begin here. Begin now.

"Caring for your own light isn't selfish.
It's what makes every other light you
tend shine brighter."

Disclaimer

Throughout this book, you'll find stories drawn from my work with clients and my own life. To respect confidentiality, names and identifying details have been changed. In some cases, stories are composites or illustrative scenarios inspired by recurring themes I've seen in my coaching practice.

Each story is shared with care — not to present a documentary record, but to illuminate the challenges, breakthroughs, and transformations that are possible for all of us.

These narratives are offered for reflection and education, not as medical, psychological, or therapeutic case studies.

PRELUDE

The Northern Light Within

An Invitation to the Season Ahead

A Note from Me to You (I'm with you in spirit, backing you)

Before we begin, I want you to hear this clearly: I am with you in spirit. I am backing you.

This is not theory, it's companionship. I am with you in these pages — through the long nights, the heavy mornings, and the quiet hours when doubt lingers. Think of this prelude as a candle lit at the door: before you step into the chapters, I want you to know you are not alone here. I've kept it simple by design — so that no matter how grey the day, you can pick it up and find something to do *right now.*

Over the years — as a life coach, writer, and once a corporate professional who has walked through his own winters — I've seen how the quietest seasons often shape us the most. My work now, through *The Calm Mind Life Coaching*, is to help others build steadiness in those seasons: to find calm not in escape, but in presence; not in perfection, but in breath.

But let's also be clear: when I speak of *winter*, I don't only mean snow and frost. Winter here is both the outer frost and the inner chill — the times when life feels stripped bare, when energy dips, when grief, burnout, or uncertainty leave you in shadow. Some winters come with ice on the branches; others arrive silently inside the chest. This book is for both.

And because it is simple, it asks two things from you: authenticity and an open mind. In today's world, social media algorithms and comparisons shape too much of what we think we like or dislike. For this season, let all of that go. Ask instead: *What defines me? What can I shed, as trees shed their leaves? What can I root more deeply, as animals prepare for storms?*

You may find ideas here you've seen before. My request is: don't just nod and scroll on. Be open to try them again. Live them. Let this winter be your laboratory of becoming. Imagine me walking with you through these pages, a quiet hand on your shoulder. (And if you want to actually reach me, you can: www.thecalmmind.co) or see the photographs at @ singhashish3 on Instagram)

This little book is a torch; you supply the flame.

Why this title (and why now)

As we travel north, away from city glare and distraction, we begin to see one of Earth's greatest shows — the northern lights. They are not sitting in the sky waiting; they are born in a moment, when charged solar winds brush the upper atmosphere and a clear, dark night allows the colours to unfold.

Our unique inner light behaves much the same. We live under the glare of screens, schedules, and self-criticism. Our glow feels hidden not because it isn't real, but because we rarely let the sky go dark. In the pause, in the clearing, in the breath, our own colours begin to move. But when we step back from the glare, clear the clutter through breath, ritual, or mindful pause, brilliance arises.

That is why this book carries the title ***The Northern Light Within.*** Winter is not just darkness; it is a canvas. Without the dark sky the aurora cannot be seen. Without silence our inner radiance remains unnoticed.

And there's another reason. This is not only about enduring winter; it is about setting the tone for everything that follows. How we meet our winters — literal and metaphorical — shapes how we greet our springs. If you can learn to shed, to reframe, and to kindle light here, you create habits that carry you far beyond these months.

Why Winter Feels Heavy

Science reminds us that winter can touch both body and mood — our systems are deeply attuned to light. As daylight withdraws:

- **Circadian rhythms** drift out of sync, making it harder to feel alert at the right times.
- **Melatonin** (the hormone that signals sleep) stays elevated longer in the morning, leaving us groggy.
- **Serotonin** (linked to mood and motivation) can drop, affecting energy and outlook.
- **Vitamin D** production in the skin declines with low sun exposure, which may influence immunity and mood.

We wake groggy. We crave carbs. We feel heavy, unmotivated, sometimes even depressed. Some of us experience the fog of Seasonal Affective Disorder, where winter's pull feels almost unbearable.

But sometimes the winter is not outside, it's inside. Chronic stress and burnout scramble our circadian rhythms just as surely as lack of light. Grief can flatten serotonin as effectively as grey skies. Loneliness can leave us craving sugar and sleep. The biology of outer winter mirrors the psychology of inner winter.

The gift of this book is that the same practices — steadying breath, nourishing food, intentional words, gratitude, and belonging — help with both kinds of winter.

Lessons from the North and beyond

Cultures who endure the harshest winters have learned not just to survive, but to create warmth and meaning inside the dark. They treat winter as a season to lean into, not to escape.

- In Iceland, despite long nights, rates of Seasonal Affective Disorder remain remarkably low — the so-called Icelandic paradox. Streets glow with candles. Families gather over fish stews rich in vitamin D. Neighbours exchange books in *Jólabókaflóð,* the "Christmas book flood." Darkness becomes cozy, cultural, connective.
- In Tromsø, Norway, residents look forward to the polar night. They ski by moonlight, gather under lanterns, and call it magical. Psychologist Kari Leibowitz has documented this positive wintertime mindset: reframing darkness as opportunity changes how the body and mind respond.
- The Sámi of Lapland relied on firelight and storytelling to carry them through months of snow.
- Inuit diets — seal, whale, preserved berries — delivered omega-3s and antioxidants long before "nutritional psychiatry" had a name.
- Festivals of light such as Diwali, Hanukkah or Christmas echo this same impulse worldwide: when darkness deepens, humans kindle brightness.

Across all of these examples runs the same pattern: **mindset + ritual + nourishment + community**. These are not just Arctic tricks; they are templates for any inner winter — practices that generate light, perspective, and resilience.

A Glimpse Northward

Imagine arriving in Tromsø in January. The sun hasn't risen for weeks; the town is blue with dusk at noon. Yet, instead of withdrawal, there's a hum of life. Children ski home from school under streetlamps. Neighbours gather over fish stew as candles flicker on the tables. Above them the aurora ripples like a green curtain. Nothing about the cold or darkness changed — what did change is how people met it. Mindset, ritual, nourishment and community turn a polar night into a living festival.

A Story Carried Through Time

Winter has always been more than weather; it is symbol and story. Across cultures and centuries, people have wrapped meaning around the dark months — not only to endure them, but to understand themselves.

In the Norse world, the light-god Baldur is struck down and the earth falls dim, yet prophecy promises his return. Renewal was always part of the story. In India, dawn rituals like Surya Namaskar greet not only the sun above but also the radiance within. The Vedas speak of the Ātman — the indwelling soul — shining brighter than a thousand suns, journeying through countless summers and winters, learning and shedding until it rests in eternal bliss. Christian mystics speak of the "light within" that darkness cannot overcome. Indigenous elders remind us that firelight is not just wood burning — it is spirit glowing in community.

If you look north, you will find the same impulse. Inuit myths tell of Malina, the sun, and Anningan, the moon, chasing each other across the sky. Even the polar night is part of an eternal rhythm, not a punishment. Families gather under lamps telling stories as medicine. These are tales, but also nervous-system practices that hold hope, repeat rhythm, and kindle inner fire. The festivals of light scattered across the globe echo this same instinct — when darkness deepens, humans kindle brightness.

Across all these stories runs one truth: humans have always learned to make their own light in dark seasons. Candles, firelight, storytelling, rituals, nourishing food — these are outer symbols of an inner capacity. They're reminders that what sustains us is not only the glow outside, but the glow we kindle within.

In summer, we think the sun will save us. In winter, we think its absence will undo us. But the real glow — the steady flame — was never outside. It was always within. Breath by breath. Word by word. Choice by choice.

A Winter of My Own and my clients

There was a winter when my own voice turned against me. A sentence repeated like a leaking tap: *"This is too much; I can't do this."* The words became weather.

I didn't just sulk. I made my wife's life hell because I couldn't handle the season; I booked overpriced getaways just to escape the darkness. Winter tantrums can cost you more than mood — they can strain love, drain money, test the foundations you care about most.

One night as frost feathered the glass, I whispered a new sentence: *"I am here. I am safe. I meet this night with enough."* At first it felt hollow. By the fifth repetition, my chest loosened. By the tenth, the room felt wider. I learned what I had taught in theory: we don't only speak words. Words speak back to us.

Clients proved this too with a nurse whispering, *"I am allowed rest."* A founder saying, *"I am enough for today."* A student shifting, *"I hate winter"* to *"I will find one thing to like today."* Their weather changed.

This isn't just poetry — it's biology, as numerous studies suggest:

- **Neuroplasticity:** repetition reshapes brain pathways.
- **RAS (reticular activating system):** your brainstem filter notices what you tell it.
- **Self-affirmation theory:** affirming values reduces stress impact.
- **Mantra, prayer, chant:** repetition as medicine across cultures.

And its simplicity itself: a few true words, paired with breath.

I came to see that winter was both a backdrop and a teacher. Everything you've just read — the science, the stories, my own struggle — leads here: an invitation to discover your northern light within.

The Invitation

Have you ever realised how lucky we are to live in cycles? For example, spring's abundance, summer's celebration, autumn's release, winter's stillness. And how lucky we are to know these cycles exist inside ourselves, too? There are times of growth, times of grief, times of rest, times of renewal.

This book is an invitation to meet winter differently. To see it not as punishment, but as a canvas. To stop postponing joy until spring, and instead to practice peace — and even delight — in the middle of the storm.

Inside you'll find:

- Science told as story.
- Rituals simple enough to practice in heavy hours.
- Cultural wisdom from those who thrive in darkness.
- Reflection prompts and pauses to anchor, shed, and grow.

Not everything will fit you. That's the point. This is a menu, not a checklist. Choose what steadies you. Return to it until it roots. Then add another. Slowly, you'll build a rhythm of clarity, kindness, light — and joy.

And when you forget — and you will — you can return again. The path is not about perfection. It is about remembering.

This is not just a book about enduring winter. It is about discovering the northern light within you — a light that does not depend on weather or circumstance. This light can be a prelude to the year ahead, kindled through perspective, ritual, and mindful choice. Use it to set your tone. Shed like the trees. Choose authenticity, openness, and a joy that doesn't wait for better weather. One breath. One word. One ritual. Simple, repeatable, powerful.

So, take a breath. Notice the room you're in. Feel the ground beneath your feet. Glimpse the quiet glow already inside you. This is where the northern light within begins — already here, already yours.

Reflection Pause

Breathe before you turn the page and ask yourself:

- What story do I usually tell about winter — outer or inner?
- What if this year, I told a different one?
- What if winter wasn't gloom, but bloom in disguise?

A Note on Positivity

Before we go any further, a truth: winter — outer or inner — can be hard. It can bring anger, frustration, guilt, grief. It can strain relationships and drain our energy. Pretending otherwise only makes it heavier.

That's why this book will never ask you to "just think positive" or to cover pain with a smile. **True positivity is not toxic positivity.** It isn't about denial or suppression. It's about *recognising, expressing, and moving through* what you feel so it no longer runs your life.

When you name a feeling — even an uncomfortable one — you've already begun to loosen its grip. When you give it space and then take one small action, you start to influence your own weather. Knowing how to navigate storms rather than avoid them is the heart of resilience.

The practices in these pages — breath, ritual, reflection, movement, words, connection — are offered as a gentle framework for exactly this. They are not quick fixes or bypasses; they are bridges. They help you express what's inside, move through it, and fill the empty space that follows with something life-giving. Over time, that turns into a rhythm where emotions no longer control you; you guide them.

This is the difference between false cheerfulness and genuine inner light. False cheerfulness closes down. Genuine inner light begins with honesty, then builds steadiness and warmth one choice at a time.

PART ONE

The Winter Loop

CHAPTER ONE

Acceptance: The First Lens of Winter

"What we accept, we stop fighting. What we stop fighting, we can finally hold."

The First Frost – When the Forest Says Yes

If the northern lights are the grand spectacle of hidden beauty, frost is its quiet whisper. It doesn't announce itself. It arrives softly — grass turned silver, breath visible in the air, trees standing in bare honesty.

Nature does not resist. Trees release their leaves with grace, conserving strength for what's unseen. Rivers slow their rush. Animals burrow or grow coats. Everything prepares — not out of fear, but wisdom.

And yet, we resist. We sigh at shorter days, mutter at the cold, rehearse our familiar lines:

"It's so dark already."
"I hate this weather."
"I can't wait for spring."

It feels harmless, but neuroscience shows complaint wires the brain toward despair. Each sigh tells the body, *this is unbearable.* The words we speak become our inner weather. And winter — outer or inner — magnifies what we speak into being.

One morning, winter arrives without asking. The sky turns pewter, silence hums in the air, and nature again demonstrates what we keep forgetting: acceptance.

The trees do not cling to their leaves, insisting, *"I will not let go."* They release them gracefully, leaving branches bare, conserving energy for the unseen labor of survival.

Animals do not protest, *"I refuse to hibernate."* They retreat into their caves, nests, and burrows, surrendering to cycles older than thought. Even rivers, once restless and rushing, do not stamp at their banks and say, *"I will not slow."* They soften their currents and carry only what is essential.

There is no bargaining in this. No bitterness. No resentment. Only a quiet, instinctive wisdom: acceptance.

Acceptance is not weakness. It is preparation. It's the invisible strength that transforms resistance into readiness. When we switch to acceptance, something remarkable happens — we move from victim to visionary, from helplessness to possibility. The brain stops looping in "why me" and starts asking "what now." That shift breaks the cycle of rumination and unlocks energy once trapped in worry — energy that can now be used for healing, clarity, and action.

And there is no better season for practising acceptance. As leaves drop from the trees, they reveal every knot and flaw in the branches. Winter takes away cushions of sunshine, leisurely walks on the beach, summer festivals and their ready-made cheer. In that stripping-back, our own coverings fall away too, revealing the places we've been hiding under busyness or brightness.

This is the true gift: winter gives you a living rehearsal space. You're not asked to love it — only to let it teach you. When you practise acceptance here — in the cold, in the absence, in the bare honesty — you build a strength that will serve you in every inner season to come.

"Peace begins the moment you stop fighting what is."

> **Reflection Prompt:** Where in your life are you still clinging to the leaves of a passing season?
> What might open if, just for today, you stopped fighting what is and began trusting what's unfolding?

Where Resistance Lives

We, unlike the forest or the stream, are experts at resisting. While trees bow under snow and rivers slow to a glassy crawl, we rail against the same rhythm of life. We mutter at the early dark, curse the snow stacking on sidewalks, groan at the cold biting through our coats. We brace ourselves as if winter were a punishment rather than a pulse, a living season asking to be met.

But resistance never changes the season; it only changes us. It tightens shoulders and clenches jaws. It keeps sleep shallow and thoughts restless. It drains our warmth, leaving us tense, brittle, and easily splintered. Our bodies fight realities that cannot be bargained with, and our minds spiral into frustration and fatigue.

Acceptance, by contrast, is not surrender. It is release. It doesn't demand that we adore every grey sky or icy morning. It simply asks us to name what is here, so our energy is no longer squandered in denial. In that naming, something softens. The sting lifts. Our minds turn from resistance to creativity and begin to ask: *What now? How might I move with this season instead of against it?*

This is where perspective begins — not in forced cheerfulness, but in the quiet, courageous choice to stop fighting what cannot be changed so you can start shaping what can. In that pause, your inner weather shifts, making space for steadiness, clarity, and even small moments of unexpected grace.

What We Can and Cannot Change

Acceptance isn't resignation; it's clarity. It's pausing long enough to see the boundary between what is yours to carry, and what is not. Weather will shift. Plans will fall through. People will move according to their own fears and hopes. Some of it will feel kind, some of it won't. All of it unfolds regardless of your opinion.

You cannot stop the snow from falling, but you can choose how you walk in it. You cannot control whether a colleague cancels a meeting, but you can shape the story you tell yourself afterward. You cannot make someone love or understand you on your timeline, but you can choose the words you speak to yourself in their silence.

When you stop struggling with what you cannot alter, you release energy for what you *can*—your breath, your posture, your rituals, the small actions that soothe and strengthen your nervous system. This is the hidden power of acceptance: it doesn't narrow your life; it concentrates your power. It is the shift from flailing in a storm to standing in a storm with your feet firmly planted, breathing until clarity returns. And from that steadiness, you not only weather what comes—you begin to grow through it.

Reflection Prompt: Write down three things this week you cannot change. Next to each, list one small response that is yours to choose–a breath, a sentence, a posture, a pause. Notice how even a tiny act changes the shape of the moment.

The Weight of Winter Words

"Ugh, it's so dark already." "I can't wait for spring." "This cold makes me miserable."

How many times have you heard those phrases tossed into conversation as soon as November arrives? Maybe you've said them yourself. They slip out like a seasonal chant we don't even notice we're repeating. At first, they seem harmless — small talk, the background noise of winter — but words are never just noise. They shape the atmosphere inside us as surely as weather shapes the sky.

Neuroscience shows that repeated words and thoughts carve grooves in the brain. The more often we echo "dark, miserable, endless," the more our nervous system believes it. Stress rises, mood dips, and suddenly the season feels heavier than it already is. It's not only the weather outside that drags us down; it's the climate of our inner dialogue.

Acceptance begins with noticing this climate. Before we reach for light therapy or comfort rituals, we can examine the language we wrap winter in. Do we call it bleak, grey, lifeless — or do we allow space for words of invitation, preparation, or even quiet beauty? That small shift isn't about forced cheerfulness; it's about freeing our attention from an old script so new possibilities can enter.

And remember — this isn't really about the weather. The practice of changing our words is the practice of changing our inner climate. Negative self-talk is its own winter: every "I can't," every "I'll never," every "This always goes wrong" lays down a layer of frost over your self-belief. Acceptance begins with a conscious pause — not resignation, but a steady breath in which you let reality land without flinching or rushing to fix it. In that small stillness, the ice inside begins to thaw and your scattered energy gathers.

Each time you meet a moment this way, you're doing more than surviving a season. You're training yourself to recognise what you cannot control and to reclaim what you can. From that steadiness you can choose your next word, your next movement, your next act of care.

This is the quiet power of acceptance: it doesn't tell you to *"just accept things as they are."* It invites you to step out of the story of blame — the endless replay of who should have, could have, or didn't. It loosens the grip of victimhood, that familiar space where energy drains into resentment and rumination.

Acceptance gives you the footing to respond wisely — not from reaction, but from grounded choice.

When resistance melts, clarity returns.
In that thaw, warmth, creativity, and resilience begin to grow — quietly at first, then steadily — not only in winter but in every season of your life.

Reflection Prompt: Pause for a moment. Write down the five words you most often use to describe winter or any problem in your life . Now ask yourself: are these words helping you bloom, or keeping you in gloom?

Acceptance Opens the Window

Acceptance opens the door; perspective is the light that walks in. When we stop demanding that winter be something else, we start seeing what it already is.

The tree, stripped bare, is no longer a symbol of loss, it is one of resilience. The snow, heavy on rooftops, is no longer an enemy, but a stage, softening edges and quieting noise. The sharp cold air, once an annoyance, awakens lungs and mind alike with its crystalline bite.

Perspective can't shorten the night, but it can soften it.

What the Camera Changed (Not the Cold)

I learned this lesson one frozen afternoon with my camera. I had resisted going outside all morning, muttering at the cold, convinced it would be misery. But then the snow fell in a way that transformed the ordinary park into something transcendent.

Overnight, the world was remade. Branches bowed under the weight of white. A forgotten bench looked like sculpture. Even the silence had grain, like film — present, tangible.

I lifted my camera, framed the shot, and forgot my hands were freezing. Shot after shot, I leaned into awe. What shifted wasn't the temperature, or the sky, or the hours of daylight. What shifted was me.

My lens reframed winter. Where I once saw hardship, I saw beauty. Where I once felt burden, I felt gift. And in that moment, I understood what nature had been modeling all along: acceptance creates the space for perspective, and perspective reveals possibility.

What the camera taught me is what whole cultures have practiced for centuries: when you change the frame, you change the season.

I began sharing these photographs on Instagram to keep myself accountable to this practice of seeing differently. Over time it became a gallery of reframing — winter, travel, and life.

The Power of Perspective

While much of the world treats winter like a season to be endured, some cultures see it as a season to be celebrated.

Inuit elders speak of winter nights not as darkness, but as a canvas for light — stars sharper than in summer, the northern lights painting the sky. Families telling stories around qulliq oil lamps, their flames flickering like stars indoors. Among Sámi communities, endurance has long woven together firelight, storytelling, joik (song), and nutrient-dense foods from land and sea — not trends, but intergenerational survival skills.

In Denmark, the philosophy of *hygge* transforms the cold into coziness. Families light candles in every window, wrap themselves in blankets, and share cake and coffee with friends. Winter becomes not a thief, but a stage for togetherness.

In Tromsø, Norway — where the sun disappears for two months — psychologist Kari Leibowitz found something remarkable. Locals didn't dread the season. They anticipated it. They spoke of it as magical. They skied under the moonlight, lit lanterns in the streets, gathered in cafes glowing like hearths. Children skated under floodlights at midnight, laughter rising in the dark.

Perspective doesn't change the length of the night. It changes the way the night feels.

Reflection Prompt: How do you usually frame winter in your own story? If you borrowed words from Tromsø or Copenhagen, what would shift?

These cultures aren't escaping winter; they are shaping it. Their rituals don't deny difficulty; they translate it into meaning.

Shedding Like the Trees

Walk through a forest in November, and you may feel an ache. The bright blaze of autumn has faded. Branches stand bare against the pale sky. At first glance, it looks like loss — a stripping away, a kind of death.

But look closer. The shedding of leaves is not weakness; it is wisdom. Leaves are fragile. In winter, they would snap under snow's weight. They would pull precious water away from the tree's core. By letting them go, the tree protects itself. It conserves energy, channels strength inward, and waits for the season when it will bloom again.

What if we did the same?

Winter isn't asking us to be less; it's asking us to be concentrated.

And it's not only leaves. We can also shed the voices inside that weigh us down. The inner critic that whispers, *"You're not enough."* The habit of resisting joy because it feels temporary. These are leaves too. Winter teaches us to let go of them as well.

> **Reflection Prompt:** What are the "leaves" you are carrying into this winter? Write three things you are ready to let go of – habits, grudges, or even expectations.

When Biology Pushes Back

Nature accepts winter instinctively. Trees shed. Rivers slow. Animals retreat into rhythm.

We, however, live at the intersection of biology and culture — and biology makes winter harder. Our chemistry, too, sheds and slows in winter — as mentioned in the prelude — serotonin falling like leaves, melatonin pooling like early dark.

Picture yourself in June. The sky begins to glow before you wake. Light slips through the curtains, a soft nudge saying, *rise — it's morning.* You stretch, already half-awake, maybe even smiling; your body feels ready, as if it had been waiting for this light all along.

Now picture January. The alarm shrieks into a black room. Your first thought: *Already?* The heaviness clings not just to your body but to your spirit. Coffee sharpens you for a moment, but the fog lingers.

That difference — between the ease of June and the weight of January — isn't laziness. It isn't weakness. It is wiring.

Our biology follows the sun. As daylight fades, our inner clocks drift. Melatonin, the hormone that invites sleep, lingers longer each morning; serotonin, the neurotransmitter that lifts mood, dips when light is scarce. Vitamin D production slows, tugging on both energy and immunity. The result: we crave sugar, move slower, think heavier.

But biology is not destiny — it is rhythm. Psychiatrist **Dr. Norman Rosenthal**, who first identified *Seasonal Affective Disorder*, showed that the same systems that dim our mood in darkness can brighten again with simple, natural interventions: morning light, movement, laughter, and a reframed perspective.

Acceptance begins here — in remembering that the fog is not your fault. Your body is not misbehaving; it's adapting to the light it's given. When melatonin drifts, light and routine help it return to balance. When serotonin dips, movement and joy refill the well.

So, when the dark morning feels impossible, pause before judgment. Whisper: *My body is recalibrating.* Open the curtains, breathe, stretch toward the faintest light. That simple act is not resistance — it is grace.

Our bodies, like tides and migrating birds, are bound to rhythms of light and dark. And if those rhythms can shift, they can also be realigned. Acceptance becomes the bridge: between the chemistry we inherit and the calm we choose.

> **Reflection Prompt:** How does winter affect your body? Which patterns feel biological, not personal? Write them down and note one supportive practice you can try this week.

If shorter days nudge our chemistry, practices can nudge it back. Acceptance becomes embodied through ritual.

Before you move on, take a breath. Notice how your body responds to light today — the angle of sun or lamp, the way your eyes soften or your shoulders ease. Is there a part of you that still resists the season? Instead of fighting it, whisper thanks to your body for adapting, for trying, for knowing what to do even when the mind forgets. *Think - What does "realignment" mean for you — not only in seasons, but in life transitions?*

Practices That Make Winter Joyful

Acceptance isn't just an idea. It becomes real only when embodied. Like trees letting go leaf by leaf, or cultures kindling firelight in the dark, we, too, need practices that turn acceptance into daily life.

Mindset begins the conversation; ritual keeps it going. The page, the meditation, the walk — each is a sentence in winter's kinder language.

Think of these practices as your "starter pack" for a steadier winter day: one ritual to shape your space (*Light Your Own Sanctuary*), one to greet the world outside (*Step into the Day*), and one to steady your inner weather when it feels heavy (*Kindling, Not Bonfires*). Together, these small acts give you both a physical and mental rhythm. They're not another to-do list; they're three doors back to calm, ready to open whenever you need them.

Lets start with the physical declutter first before we move to some acceptance rituals for the mind that make us accept the longer nights and the freeze with ease and a different perspective

Physical Acceptance - Decluttering as Shedding

How to practice:

1. Choose one drawer, one shelf, or one closet at a time.
2. Ask of each object: *Does this support me in this season? Or is it a burden?*
3. Release gently. Donate what can help others, recycle what can be renewed, discard what cannot.

Why it works:

Clutter is resistance made visible. Every object we no longer use but keep "just in case" is a leaf we refuse to shed. Neuroscience shows clutter heightens stress and drains focus. Decluttering mirrors nature's wisdom: letting go of the unnecessary to conserve energy for what matters.

What you may feel:

At first, discomfort — the tug of attachment. But soon after, a lightness. Space opening not just in your home, but in your mind. Every cleared surface is a bare branch — ready for new light.

> **Reflection Prompt**: Walk through your home this week and list three areas that feel heavy with clutter. Which one will you clear as your "winter shedding" ritual?

Light Your Own Sanctuary (A Winter Festival of Light)

How to practise:

1. Pick one corner of your home to become a small sanctuary. Add light — candles, string lights, lanterns. Add warmth — a blanket, cushions, a favourite chair.

2. Personalise it with objects that make you feel at home: a photo, a talisman, a scrap of fabric, a memento from a trip.
3. Once a week (or more), switch off electric lights at sunset. Light your candles or lanterns and sit with the glow for an hour. Read, write, breathe or simply rest.

Why it works:
Environment shapes mood; light and colour act on the nervous system. Across cultures winter rituals — Diwali lamps, Hanukkah menorahs, Christmas trees, *hygge* in Denmark — exist because humans instinctively create light in darkness. This isn't decoration; it's self-regulation and connection to something older than yourself.

What you may feel:
Comfort, safety, a quiet sense of sacredness. Winter becomes less something pressing against you and more something you can shape. A slowing down that feels both restful and reverent.

> **Reflection Prompt:** List three objects or symbols that spark warmth or meaning for you. How could you weave them into your winter space so that, when you sit in candlelight, you're sitting inside your own story?

Step into the Day (Outdoor Ritual)

How to practise:
1. Within an hour of waking, step outside for at least 10 minutes. No sunglasses if comfortable; let your eyes meet the open sky.
2. On harsh days, stand at a window or doorway and practise a one-minute "sky meditation" to track a cloud, a branch, or a single flake as it moves, then return to your breath.

3. Pair it with a warm cue — tea, a favourite song, a short stretch — so the ritual feels inviting rather than another task.

Why it works:
Morning daylight anchors your circadian rhythm and lifts winter mood by nudging melatonin earlier and supports serotonin production and balance. Even on cloudy days, outdoor light is many times brighter than indoor light. Across traditions, stepping out at dawn was a way to honour renewal — from Vedic *Surya Namaskar* to Japanese *asa geiko* (morning practice) — greeting not just the sun above but the vitality within.

What you may feel:
A gentle "click" of alertness. Clearer focus mid-morning. Over time, steadier afternoon energy and a quiet sense that you've met the day rather than hidden from it.

> **Reflection Prompt:** Where could ten minutes of light fit most easily in your mornings this week? If you tried it for seven days, what small difference would you hope to notice?

Mental acceptance

Language as Weather (Reframing Weather Talk)

How to practice:
1. Notice when you or others complain about the cold/dark.
2. Experiment with alternate phrases:
   - Instead of "It's so depressing," try "It's a chance to slow down."
   - Instead of "It's freezing," try "The air is crisp, it wakes me up."
   - Instead of "I can't wait for spring," try "I'm curious what winter will show me this week."

Why it works:
Words matter. Complaints reinforce gloom. Reframing weather language can shift mood — both yours and the person you're speaking with.

What you may feel:
Resistance at first. It may feel artificial. But over time, the brain learns new grooves, new associations. Language becomes a doorway to resilience.

> **Reflection Prompt:** Write three alternate sentences you can use this week when describing the weather. Practice them out loud. Notice how your body feels when you say them.

Pages That Hold the Storm (Vent-it-Out Journaling) – a must do as its akin to the physical decluttering

How to practice:
1. Keep a notebook or pad dedicated only to winter rants or in general any rants
2. Each evening, write one page of what you disliked that day — the slush, the cold, the grey. Don't edit. Don't censor.
3. When the page is full, close the book. Leave it there.

Why it works:
When we keep complaints and irritations inside, they swirl in loops, amplifying stress. Writing is a transfer of energy — moving negativity from body to page. Neuroscience confirms that expressive writing lowers stress and eases rumination.

What you may feel:
Relief. Sometimes laughter at your own exaggerations. Over time, the irritations lose their grip because they have a place to live — outside of you.

> **Reflection Prompt:** After a week, look back at your vent pages. Do you notice patterns? Are the same things bothering you, or do they shift?

Kindling, Not Bonfires (Small Sparks of Light)

How to practise:

1. Begin your day by naming its weight honestly: "Some days are heavy. That's allowed."
2. Instead of forcing yourself into cheer, pick one small, realistic spark:
   - Laugh at a short sitcom clip instead of scrolling bad news.
   - Light a candle instead of cursing the dark.
   - Journal frustrations instead of bottling them.
   - Take a five-minute walk at noon, even if the sky is pewter.
3. Treat each act as kindling — one small stick placed on the fire of your day.

Why it works:

Toxic positivity demands bonfires of constant cheer; acceptance offers you a match and a handful of sticks. Neuroscience shows that micro-choices (even two–five minutes) helps gently shift mood. Enough small sticks create fire.

What you may feel:

Relief from the pressure to "be positive." A quiet sense of agency. Over time, these small sparks gather into a steadier inner fire that naturally supports deeper practices like meditation.

> **Reflection Prompt:** What is one tiny choice you can make tomorrow morning that would set a different tone for your day? Write it down and commit to it for a week.

The Northern Light Within

Acceptance is preparation in disguise — a quieter kind of strength.

When trees shed their leaves, they are not giving up; they are getting ready. When cultures kindle fire and light, they are not denying the night — they are reminding themselves that darkness is never final.

So too with you. This winter, you do not need to carry every burden. You do not need to fight every shadow. You need only to meet the season as it is — to shed what you cannot carry, and to choose small rituals that kindle your own northern light within.

This book uses winter as its canvas, but the brushstrokes reach wider — into how we meet resistance, soften into what is, and reframe not only the cold months but the inner winters of doubt, fatigue, and fear.

To accept winter is to learn a new language of self-kindness — less resistance, more compassion, more readiness to bloom quietly in the dark.

Pause here. Close your eyes. Inhale slowly, and whisper — not as instruction, but as remembrance:

I accept the season. I accept myself. I am ready to bloom in winter.

CHAPTER ONE SUMMARY - ACCEPTANCE AS PREPARATION

Key Insight

Nature does not resist winter. Trees shed leaves, animals hibernate, rivers slow. Acceptance is not resignation – it is wisdom, conservation, and preparation. The same applies to our lives: resistance drains us, acceptance frees us to adapt.

Core Metaphors

- Trees Shedding: letting go of burdens, habits, grudges.
- Indigenous Fires & Stories: warmth and connection as survival.
- Scandinavian Mindset: hygge, mysig, friluftsliv → reframing winter as opportunity.

Rituals of Acceptance

- Decluttering as Shedding – release items that weigh you down; clearing outside reflects clearing within.
- Vent-it-Out Journaling – release winter complaints onto paper, not into your body.
- Decorating with Joy – create one sanctuary corner with light, warmth, and personal touches.
- Reframing Weather Talk – replace "bleak and depressing" with "slowing down" or "crisp and awakening."

Reflection Prompts:

- What do I usually resist each winter? How could I reframe it as preparation?
- What "leaves" (habits, grudges, clutter) am I ready to shed this season?
- Write three alternate sentences you can use when describing winter weather.

Closing Meditation Mantra

"I accept the season. I accept myself. I am ready to bloom in winter."

CHAPTER TWO

Openness:
The Second Breath of Winter

"Every yes is a doorway. Step through it, and the room gets bigger."

From Acceptance to Openness

Acceptance is the first pause — the unclenching of the fist, the steady breath that says, *I will stop fighting what is here.* But pausing alone doesn't guarantee movement. You may have stopped resisting the outer situation yet still be resisting on the inside. Old beliefs, biases, and conditioning run like background programs, shaping how you interpret the moment. They whisper, *Nothing good ever happens here,* or *I've seen this before; it always ends badly.* Without noticing, you're standing at the threshold with the door unlocked but your hand still on the knob.

This is why acceptance is not the finish line but the opening gate. It clears the noise enough for you to hear the subtler barriers within yourself. When you bring curiosity to those inner patterns — noticing, questioning, gently loosening them — you begin to create the conditions for a true shift. The mind's energy, once locked in its old grooves, becomes available for fresh thinking, new choices, creative problem solving.

Openness isn't passive; it's a deliberate practice of making room for what your conditioning would normally block. It's the willingness to ask, *What if my assumptions aren't the whole story? What else could emerge here?* In that space, solutions you couldn't imagine while bracing against the problem begin to surface — not because the situation changed, but because you did.

The Most Common Barrier I See

Again and again, I see this in clients: they want to change but some invisible weight keeps pulling them back. Old traumas, old verdicts, old self-talk or sometimes simply the weight of our ego— frayed, heavy, but familiar — become a barrier between them and the life they long for. They clutch misery like an old blanket because, at some level, it feels safer than the unknown. Acceptance helps them set it down. But openness is what allows them to take a step without it — to feel the raw air on their skin and discover it doesn't destroy them. That's where freedom begins. On many occasions I have allowed my old beliefs, habits, and conditioning to open and change the mindset.

Another layer of this barrier is time itself. We don't only carry memories of the past; we build our vision of the future from those memories. We project yesterday's hurts onto tomorrow's blank page and call it prediction. Our minds loop between old pain and imagined disappointment, creating a false certainty: *This is how it always goes.* That loop can feel like realism but it's really resistance — a self-reinforcing map that leaves no space for new roads.

This is why two people can stand in the same winter and live in different worlds. One collapses inward, replaying the same script: "Nothing helps. I can't change." The nights lengthen around them, the dark presses closer. Another whispers, "What if this time is different?" They do some calming breaths. They write a few lines before bed. They step outside to feel the hush of snow beneath stars. Their world expands, even in the same cold.

That's what I want you to do through this book. You may have heard some of these ideas before, and some of them might not have worked for you in the past. But how about being more open this time, and try them again with a freer mind? Sometimes it begins with nothing more than a sentence spoken quietly to yourself: *"I am open to a new idea."* Or *"I am open to trying that old idea again — but with a freer mind this time."* Tiny phrases like these are invitations; they create a crack in the old pattern and let fresh air in. They work like small spells, shifting your nervous system from guardedness to possibility.

The difference is not the weather. It's the willingness to open — to stop using the past as a forecast, to loosen the grip of old patterns, and to give the future a chance to arrive unfiltered. In that openness, change stops being a theory and starts becoming an experience.

> **Reflection Prompt:** Where in your own life do you confuse *"breaking down"* with *"breaking open"*? What would it mean to see the cracks not as evidence of failure, but as entry points for light?

Clearing the Room

Openness begins with making space. Neuroscience tells us that memory is not a static file but a living network. Every time we recall an event, we slightly rewrite it, strengthening some pathways and pruning others. Habits and beliefs are built the same way: through repetition. Without realising it, we turn the past into furniture, arranging our mental room with boxes labelled *failure, success, never again, always like this.* There's barely room to move, let alone bring in something new.

Psychologist Daniel Kahneman puts it simply: *"Nothing in life is as important as you think it is while you are thinking about it."* We forget this when we're living inside our own mental clutter. Most of us never stop to unlock the door. We keep inhabiting the echo of old moments and mistake it for the whole world.

Clearing space doesn't mean throwing everything away at once. It means turning the key, letting in light, and looking honestly at what's inside. Which stories are still true? Which habits have become junk? Which "truths" were only assumptions you outgrew long ago? This is not self-blame; it's self-housekeeping. Without this clearing, even the best new idea has nowhere to land.

Our conditioning, our past failures, and even our past victories can crowd the present. We hold on to "this didn't work" or "this always works" so tightly that we can't experiment. Acceptance of the present — of what's actually here, right now — is the door handle. Openness is the act of stepping inside with clear eyes and fresh air.

When you make space, you give possibility a place to sit. In that cleared room, the same practices you've tried before can work differently, because you are different. Your nervous system is no longer on guard; it's ready to learn. That is when change stops being a concept and starts becoming a living experience.

Reflection Prompt: Picture the "room" of your mind. What's the heaviest box you keep dragging from the past into the future? What small action could you take this week to open it or set it down?

Breaking Open

When we begin clearing the room of the mind, what we uncover isn't always neat. Sometimes the clutter we touch first is a story we've been carrying so long it feels like part of our body.

I once worked with a woman whose story was so heavy it shaped her every step. Each year, as the season shifted, she would say almost as a ritual: *"This is when I break."* She wasn't describing a moment; she was predicting it. Her words had become a spell she cast over her own life. Her shoulders curved inward as if protecting a heart too fragile to risk the air. Her breath stayed shallow. Her eyes dimmed — not because the world was dark, but because she no longer expected to see light. She lived in absolutes: always, never, nothing. These weren't sentences anymore; they were shackles.

One day I asked her, gently but directly: *"What if this isn't breaking you down? What if it's breaking you open?"* She looked at me as if I had spoken a language she didn't know. But the question stayed. Like a seed tucked under frost, it began to stir in silence.

At first, the change was imperceptible. She bought a small notebook and began scribbling jagged lines — not insights, just fragments: sighs, single words, half-prayers. She allowed herself, for the first time in years, to nap in the afternoon without condemning herself for weakness. Rest became less of a crime, more of a kindness. Then, one evening, she pulled out a box of paints she hadn't touched in years. Her hand trembled as she dipped the brush. When the colour spread across the canvas, her eyes softened. Something inside had cracked — not broken apart, broken open.

Her world did not instantly bloom into spring. The same season, the same night, now carried possibility. What once haunted her began to hold her.

This is the nature of openness. It rarely arrives like lightning; it leaks through cracks. It doesn't demand a grand transformation; it begins with the smallest yes. A notebook opened. A nap taken without guilt. A trembling brushstroke that whispers: *I am willing.*

And isn't that true of all our winters — the external ones that shorten days, and the internal ones that hollow us? What feels like breaking down may also be breaking open, if we dare to see the cracks not as ruins but as the first paths for light.

Sometimes what feels like breaking down is just the sound of a shell cracking open.

The Languages of Openness

Her story is not unique. Across centuries and cultures, humans have wrestled with the same truth: how do we open when everything in us longs to close? Each tradition has its own language for this — but together, they form a chorus.

Yoga: The Posture of the Heart

In yoga, openness begins with *śoshana* — loosening. The unwinding of rigidity, the softening of what has become too tight. Only in that loosening does *ānanda* — bliss — appear. It is not an easy bliss. It demands vulnerability.

Consider the backbends: the bow, the camel, the wheel. In each, the body curves into space it cannot see. The ribs stretch wide, the heart arches open, the throat is exposed. These postures are acts of trust: you cannot cling, you cannot fold inward, you must yield. You cannot perform them with clenched fists or tight shoulders. The body must first release to allow. To be open is to bow back into life, heart exposed, trusting the space in front of you.

Life asks the same of us. To live with openness is to bow back into life itself, heart exposed, trusting the space in front of you. This is not comfort — it is courage. And every time you dare to do it, whether on a mat or in a moment of honesty, you practice the discipline of opening.

Where in your own life are you still folding in, shoulders hunched, heart shielded? What would it mean to straighten, to soften, to risk openness instead?

The Greek Mirror: Demeter and Persephone

The Greeks told this truth in myth. When Persephone descended into the underworld, her mother Demeter's grief closed the world. Crops withered, soil hardened, the earth froze barren. This is what happens when loss hardens into rigidity: the world inside us stops growing.

But the story did not end there. Persephone returned. Not fully, not forever — but cyclically. Half the year lost, half restored. Demeter had to learn not only to grieve the absence, but to reopen to the return. Only then did spring emerge.

The lesson is not myth alone. Every one of us knows the cycle: grief arrives, and we close. Joy knocks, and we resist it, fearing its impermanence. Yet openness is not denial of loss. It is the courage to let joy return, even when sorrow still has a seat at the table.

Like Demeter, we must learn to live not only in absence, but in return — to let joy step back into the room. Change and joy rarely arrive all at once. They come in drops, in glimpses, in seasons. If you slam the door because it's "not enough yet," you miss the first shoots of growth. Openness means welcoming even those small drops of return. Let them land. Let them accumulate. In time, they become a tide.

What joy have you kept outside the door because grief arrived first? Can you open the door, even knowing joy may not stay forever?

The Inuit Fire: Connection in the Dark

Far north, the Inuit faced winters that swallowed the sun for months. Survival demanded more than calories. It demanded openness to what remained. And so they gathered. Around drum dances, around stories, around laughter. They did not treat the dark as enemy. They turned it into canvas.

Modern science now tells us why it worked: oxytocin, the bonding hormone, rises in shared ritual. But the Inuit already knew this. Firelight gave warmth, but story gave belonging. Connection reopened what cold and dark tried to close.

We live with our own long nights — depression, heartbreak, exhaustion, fear. In those winters, isolation whispers to us: "Close off, endure alone." But the Inuit remind us that the medicine is not isolation, it's connection. To light a fire — literal or figurative — and share it.

Who are the voices you can gather with, even in your own dark season? What would it mean to treat your night not as an enemy, but as a place for story, for song, for belonging?

A Shared Truth

Yoga, Greek myth, Inuit ritual — three different worlds, one shared truth: openness is not passive. It is not waiting for light to return on its own. It is the active courage to bend, to return, to connect.

It is the posture of the heart. It is the permission for joy. It is the fire that keeps us alive.

Reflection Prompt: Which "language" of openness speaks most to you right now – the posture of the heart, the myth of return, or the circle of fire? How might you practice that language this week?

Gentle Practices of Openness

Openness is not achieved once; it is rehearsed. Every day, the world tempts you to fold back into the familiar, to protect yourself by closing. Openness isn't a switch you flip once; it's a discipline practiced in small gestures. For thousands of years, people in harsh climates, monasteries, temples, and long winters have used tiny rituals to stay soft when everything around them urged them to harden.

These are not chores. They are rehearsals — ancient gestures renewed in your own hands. Small, repeatable, everyday acts that train your nervous system to stay open and soft even when life asks you to shrink. Saying, "I can stay open even now" is not a single heroic act. It is a posture we practice, like breathing or walking when the world tempts us to fold back into the familiar, to protect ourselves by closing.

• The Yes Experiment

Long before self-help books, cultures found ways to say yes in the face of dark months. Inuit families danced and drummed in communal halls when silence seemed easier. Norwegians in Tromsø said yes to skiing under a moonlit sky. Yogis bow into postures they cannot see, heart exposed, trusting the space ahead.

This week, choose one small "yes" where you usually default to "no." Yes to a walk when the sky looks dull. Yes to a conversation you usually avoid.

Yes to tasting a new spice. The yes need not be dramatic; its power lies in being deliberate. Why it works: Every time you override a habitual "no," you teach your nervous system that novelty is not threat. Small yeses expand your world without overwhelming it. They gently widen your tolerance for joy and change.

Every yes is a doorway. Step through it, and the room gets bigger. Rigidity is built on no. No to risk, no to discomfort, no to the unknown. But every no is also a wall.

• The Posture of Openness

The body carries your stories before your words do. Arms folded, shoulders hunched, gaze lowered — this is the body's way of saying, *"I am closed."*

Now try the opposite. Straighten your spine. Let your shoulders fall back. Open your chest as though you were receiving light. This is not cosmetic. It is neurological. When the body opens, the nervous system relaxes, perspective widens.

Sometimes the heart cannot open until the body does first.

Across traditions, posture carries meaning: monks open their palms when praying, yogis arch their hearts to the sky, elders stand at firesides with chests lifted to receive heat. The body signals "safe" before the mind believes it.

When life feels heavy, we fold in — arms crossed, shoulders hunched, breath shallow. Pause and try the opposite. Plant your feet. Roll your shoulders back. Let your chest lift as if receiving light. Why it works: Body language feeds the brain. When you open the chest and lift the gaze, you stimulate the vagus nerve, and increase a sense of safety. Sometimes the heart cannot open until the body does first.

"Train the body to open, and the heart will learn to follow."

• The Beginner's Gesture

Zen calls it *shoshin* — "beginner's mind." Old Norse farmers spoke of the first snow as "new eyes on old land." Both point to the same truth: novelty softens rigidity.

Rigidity thrives on repetition without awareness — the same path to work, the same words in conversation, the same reflexes under stress. Openness can be cultivated by interrupting this autopilot.

Choose one ordinary act — making tea, stepping outside, brushing your teeth — and approach it as if for the first time. Notice textures, sounds, sensations. You're not just performing a habit; you're waking up inside it.

Why it works: Familiarity dulls awareness and tightens patterns. Seeing the ordinary as new interrupts autopilot, lowers stress hormones, and opens creative circuits in the brain. It is a micro-practice in presence, a daily rehearsal for openness.

You can also add one small element to your day that feels like an opening: play music you've never heard, stand for two minutes at a window letting the horizon stretch your gaze, breathe differently before you speak. What matters is not the ritual itself but the intention behind it:

I am practicing spaciousness and clearing makes room; opening invites what is new to enter.

Remember -

These practices are not chores. They are training grounds. Each one is a refusal to close, a rehearsal for joy. Done once, they may feel trivial. Done daily, they reshape you. Choose what aligns with you the best.

Here is the truth: winter is not testing you to see if you can endure. It is training you to see if you can open.

Closing Reflection – Seeds Beneath the Snow

Openness is the soil. It is the quiet cracking of the shell, the discipline of staying soft when everything tempts you to harden, and the courage to loosen old stories so new roots can form. But soil alone is not enough. It must be fed.

A seed can split, but if there is no light, no water, no nourishment, it withers before it grows. So it is with us. Acceptance loosens our grip; openness clears the ground. Yet even then, our old habits, biases and predictions can drift back like frost, seeding the same patterns unless we choose what to plant next. Once we have dared to open, the question becomes: *what are we feeding ourselves in that openness?*

Because whether we notice it or not, we are always feeding. Food that steadies the body. Stories that saturate the mind. Rituals that either soothe or scatter the spirit. Words we whisper to ourselves about who we are and what's possible. Winter, stripped bare, makes this truth visible. It shows us what we're truly consuming, and how that quiet diet builds or depletes us.

This is the hidden power of openness: it's not just the absence of resistance; it's a space where you can plant something new. A simple inner phrase — *"I am open to a new idea"* or *"I am open to trying that old idea again with a freer mind"*— is like scattering fresh seed. Each small sentence is an invitation that cracks the old pattern, lets fresh air in, and shifts your nervous system from guardedness to possibility.

Openness prepares the ground. Nourishment decides the harvest.

In the next chapter we'll gather at the winter table. Not only to talk about what we eat, but what we consume in every sense: the meals on our plates, the stories on our screens, the beliefs we rehearse in silence. For body, mind, and spirit each have their own hunger. And winter, perhaps more than any other season, asks you: *what are you feeding?*

CHAPTER TWO SUMMARY - OPENNESS: THE SECOND BREATH OF WINTER

Key Insight

Acceptance loosens the grip; openness lets the light in. Where acceptance ends resistance, openness begins movement. It is the discipline of staying soft when everything tempts you to harden – of saying a small, deliberate *yes* to life's unknowns. Each act of openness is a rehearsal for courage and creativity.

Core Metaphors

- Clearing the Room: making space in the mind so new ideas and perspectives can enter.
- Breaking Open: the cracks that appear under pressure can be entry points for light.
- Posture of the Heart (Yoga): loosening and trusting the space in front of you.
- Demeter & Persephone (Greek Myth): learning to reopen to return and renewal.
- Inuit Fire: connection and story as warmth and belonging in the dark.

Rituals of Openness

- The Yes Experiment – choose one small, intentional *yes* where you'd normally say no. Every yes is a doorway; step through it and the room gets bigger.
- The Posture of Openness – lift your spine, drop your shoulders, open your chest to light. When the body opens, the heart follows.
- The Beginner's Gesture – bring fresh attention to ordinary acts; novelty softens rigidity and rekindles presence.

Reflection Prompts

- Where in your life do you confuse *breaking down* with *breaking open*?
- What old story, assumption, or habit is crowding the "room" of your mind?
- Which "language" of openness speaks most to you – the posture of the heart, the myth of return, or the circle of fire?

Closing Meditation Mantras

"I am open to new ideas.
I am open to what returns.
I am open to light finding me, even here."

"Every yes is a doorway. Step through it, and the room gets bigger."

CHAPTER THREE

Nourishment : Feeding Body, Mind, and Spirit

"Nourishment is not just food on the plate, but the stories and silence we serve ourselves daily."

By now you've practiced softening resistance and opening a little space. Think of that space as soil under frost — inner soil. What you feed it next decides what will grow when the thaw comes, whether that thaw is springtime or simply the easing of an anxious period.

Winter is our metaphor for any season of contraction: a job loss, a heartbreak, a bout of burnout, a stretch of self-doubt. In those inner winters we can't always change the weather, but we can choose what we take in. Food, yes — but also news, conversations, self-talk, screens, stories, rituals. Every input is a form of nourishment or depletion.

Across cultures, long nights have always been met with deliberate feeding — not only stews for the body but myths for the imagination, candles for the spirit. These weren't quaint customs; they were nervous-system medicine. They still are.

This chapter is about that medicine. About asking, *"Now that I've accepted what is, now that I've opened a little space, what do I want to pour into that space?"* Not to force cheerfulness, not to slap on "positive vibes," but to make conscious, sustaining choices in a time when passivity and autopilot would otherwise take over.

We'll look at three layers — body, mind, and spirit — and simple ways to nourish each. Only after we've explored the mind section will I invite you to examine your digital diet and screen time as part of that nourishment. For now, simply hold this thought: *what I consume shapes my inner climate as much as the outer weather does.*

> **Reflection Prompts:** Before moving on, take a breath. Think of a time you went through your own "winter." Without judging, jot down three things you naturally turned to for comfort. They might be foods, routines, people, or thoughts. Which of them truly sustained you?

Feeding the Body: Warmth as a First Language

When nights grow long — whether outside your window or inside your heart — the body feels it first. Fatigue arrives before sadness, cravings before clarity. This is not a moral failing; it's biology. Less light means less serotonin, more melatonin, slower rhythms. We reach for quick fuel because the nervous system is quietly asking for comfort. In winter, everything slows — metabolism, movement, even mood. We instinctively turn to food for comfort: soups, stews, warm bread, spiced teas. But nourishment is never just about calories or vitamins. It's about what we feed our body, yes — but also what we feed our *mind* and *spirit.*

Cultures who have endured hard winters never treated food as a side note. They treated it as the first language of care. In the north, families gather around soups and stews rich with protein and omega-3s long before science could name them. In mountain villages, people bake dense breads that stay warm under cloth all morning. Even festival sweets — from Diwali laddoos to Christmas puddings — evolved not only to celebrate, but to store energy and brighten dark months with spice and ritual.

Feeding yourself well in your own winter works the same way. It isn't about rules or punishment. It's about asking: *"What would steady me?"* Maybe that's a bowl of soup at lunch instead of a sugar rush at 3 p.m. Maybe it's actually eating breakfast before the first email. Maybe it's making one warm drink a small ceremony instead of gulping coffee between tasks.

You're not only refuelling your cells. You're sending your nervous system a message: *I'm safe, I'm cared for, I'm not rushing.* A warm meal or drink can become a micro-ritual — a pause that grounds you before you head back into the day.

> **Reflection Prompt:** Think back to a time you felt worn down. What food, drink, or simple preparation actually comforted you rather than just distracted you? How might you weave one such "steadying" ritual into your winter mornings or afternoons this week?

Part One: Food for the Body – Ancient Wisdom, Modern Clarity

Nourishment in the North

Every seed that opens asks the same thing: *feed me, or I cannot grow.* Our ancestors understood this with instinctive clarity. In winter, food was never just a meal. It was survival, medicine, mood stabilizer, and ritual in one.

- **The Inuit**, wrapped in Arctic darkness, ate fatty fish and seal fat — brimming with omega-3s and Vitamin D — centuries before science proved they guard against depression and inflammation. They even preserved berries in fat, hiding summer's light inside winter's night.
- **In Iceland**, cod liver oil was more than a supplement. It was a morning ritual, a spoonful of resilience. It brightened moods, strengthened bones, and became a cultural memory: *this is how we greet the day.*
- **The Sámi herders of Lapland** leaned on reindeer meat and long-simmered stews. Around the fire, nourishment was not only eaten; it was shared, binding people together in warmth.
- **In India's Ayurveda**, winter foods were chosen to ground and fortify — ghee, ginger, turmeric, lentils, root vegetables. Recipes doubled as reminders: in seasons of depletion, eat what strengthens, not what scatters.

Different climates, different traditions — but the same truth: food is more than fuel. It is chemistry, culture, and a covenant with life. In every seed, in every human being, growth depends on what is given inside.

The Modern Winter Plate

We may not be living as hunter-gatherers or tending fires in Lapland, but the principles still apply. What you put on your plate today directly shapes your resilience tomorrow. You don't have to overhaul your diet; you can borrow one element at a time:

- **Omega-3s**: salmon, mackerel, trout, walnuts, flaxseeds → natural mood stabilizers.
- **Vitamin D**: mushrooms, fortified dairy, or supplements when needed → essential in darker latitudes.
- **Complex carbs**: oats, lentils, quinoa, brown rice → help the brain produce serotonin, the "feel-good" chemical.
- **Citrus and greens**: spinach, kale, oranges, lemons → boosting immunity and vitality.

- Spices: ginger, turmeric, cinnamon → warming the body and calming inflammation.

Practice – The Winter Mood Bowl

Once a week, create a bowl built on this template:

- Base: quinoa, oats, or rice.
- Protein: salmon, lentils, or chicken.
- Healthy fat: avocado, olive oil, or walnuts.
- Colour: citrus slices, spinach, or berries.

Before eating, pause. Look at the bowl. Whisper: *This is sunlight in another form.*

Author's Note

As you finish this section, a quick reminder: **I'm not a certified dietitian or medical professional.** What you've just read is drawn from research and practices that have helped me and many of my clients, but it is not meant as personalised medical advice.

Each body is unique; your needs may differ based on health conditions, medications, culture, or lifestyle. Use what resonates, adapt what you need, and speak with a qualified professional if you're unsure. Think of the above section as a framework — a menu of ideas to support you — rather than a prescription.

The Science of Food and Mood

Modern research is catching up with what traditions always knew: diet is not neutral — it shapes the nervous system.

- Professor Felice Jacka's research, including the SMILES Trial, suggests that a shift toward whole foods and balanced nutrition can meaningfully lift mood and support recovery from depression.
- Nutritionist Jerlyn Jones, RDN, highlights how lean proteins, berries, Vitamin B12, and Vitamin D-rich foods specifically buffer winter mood dips.
- Studies on the gut–brain axis reveal how the microbiome — nourished by fiber, fermented foods, and plant diversity — communicates with the brain, influencing anxiety, resilience, and overall mood.

Put simply: a body fed with stable, nutrient-rich foods produces a mind that is steadier, calmer, and more resilient.

Reflection Reflection:

- What foods dominate your winter plate right now?
- Which leave you sluggish, and which leave you energized?
- Which one new "mood food" can you commit to adding this week?

"Food fuels the body.
But it also steadies the mind."

Part Two - Food for the Mind
The Table We Don't Notice

Every seed needs more than soil and water. It needs atmosphere — the air around it, the conditions that whisper, *grow here.* For us, that atmosphere is our mental diet. What we feed our minds becomes the weather in which our lives either wither or thrive.

In winter, this becomes sharper. The world outside is stripped bare, so what we consume inside stands out. Our ancestors knew this. Every spoonful of stew, every preserved berry, every story around the fire was chosen with care. Food fed the body, but story fed the mind.

Today, our "winter table" looks very different. We are not only eating meals. We are consuming headlines, reels, conversations, songs, shows, and comment threads. Some feed us. Many drain us.

The tragedy is that we rarely notice. We'll worry about sugar, gluten, or caffeine, but not about the steady snack of outrage politics. We'll count calories but not the endless calories of fear and comparison served up by our phones. We'll talk about healthy eating but not healthy listening.

And yet — the body doesn't care whether it's sugar or a toxic headline. Both raise our stress levels. Both unsettle sleep. Both leave us craving more of what depletes us.

Every bite and every scroll is a choice: to nourish, or to drain.

Just as you can't control the length of the night, you can still choose the warmth of the room you sit in. You cannot change every event, but you can choose how you meet it, what you allow in, and what you quietly set aside.

One of my clients used to tell me, "I don't have time for rituals." I asked her to check her phone's screen-time report. She laughed out loud when she saw it — hours spent on news feeds that left her more anxious, not more informed. She didn't shame herself; she just swapped ten minutes of scrolling for ten minutes of reading something nourishing. Within a week, her mood shifted. Not a miracle — a small, conscious re-feeding of the mind.

Just like food, your mental intake does not need a total overhaul. It needs small, deliberate substitutions — one story for another, one conversation for another. Over time, those small choices change the climate inside you.

Reflection Prompt: When you picture your own "winter table," what is served most often – nourishing meals and stories, or endless streams of noise and chatter? Write down one input you want to eat more of, and one you're ready to push aside.

Dark Chatter: The Junk Food of the Mind

Here's the truth: most of us snack all day on digital junk food — not with our mouths, but with our minds.

It looks like this:

The News and Outrage buffet

It begins innocently — one headline while sipping coffee. Then another. Then a third. Before you realize it, you've wandered into the comment section, watching strangers argue in all caps.

None of it involves you, yet your body doesn't know that. Your shoulders inch upward. Your breath turns shallow. Your chest tightens. By the time you look up, the coffee is cold, your morning energy is gone, and your nervous system is primed for battle. What began as *staying informed* has become a steady drip of adrenaline — a storm you never consented to walk into. Sometimes that storm arrives disguised as care. It lands in your inbox or group chat wrapped in concern — a forwarded video, a "just sharing" post, a breaking-news clip. You open it casually, meaning no harm. Within seconds, your pulse quickens. Someone's shouting. Someone's blaming. Your mind starts sprinting though you haven't moved an inch.

And then come the reels — ten seconds of curated chaos. A tragedy becomes a trend. A cause becomes a slogan. Your feed becomes a carousel of reactions — anger, pity, envy, fatigue — none of which belong to you, yet all of which live in your body. Even compassion turns corrosive when it's served without pause. Politics, too, has mastered this rhythm. Each post claims truth, each headline demands allegiance. The algorithm amplifies extremes, shrinking the middle ground until it disappears. And between hashtags and hot takes, you begin to mistake reaction for responsibility — outrage for awareness.

Outrage is the junk food of awareness — spicy, addictive, and briefly satisfying. It tricks the brain into feeling involved while quietly draining its calm. Hours later, long after you've scrolled away, a residue remains — a faint bitterness, a restlessness you can't trace back to its source. That's the true cost of outrage: not the seconds you spent reading it, but the serenity you spend recovering from it. And here's the deeper truth: **the machine knows this.** Every click, every heartbeat, every hesitation teaches it what hooks you — especially what provokes you. The algorithm has learned that fear spreads faster than joy, that outrage holds attention longer than peace. Negativity sells better. Calm rarely trends. So it keeps feeding you storms — not to inform you, but to keep you scrolling, quietly feeding your fears and your biases alike. What feels like curiosity is often conditioning. What seems like awareness is sometimes agitation in disguise. And when the outrage fades, another hunger takes its place — the quieter storm of comparison.

The Comparison Platter

You open Instagram "just for a minute." A minute becomes fifteen. Fifteen becomes a quiet erosion. By the time you look up, you're certain everyone else has a better body, a cleaner house, a more exciting life. It's the snack that leaves you starving.

But here's what we forget: you're not comparing lives — you're comparing edits. The feed isn't a mirror; it's a museum of highlights curated to look like truth. A smiling picture does not mean a smiling life. Often, behind that frozen image is a private storm no one else can see. There were winters when people saw my photos — a calm smile, a serene landscape — and assumed I was thriving.

But behind the lens, I was hurting. Fighting exhaustion. Carrying private fears. The camera caught the mask, not the ache beneath it. And still, people compared themselves to that mask — just as I have compared myself to others.

That's what comparison really does: it takes your unfiltered life and measures it against someone else's carefully chosen fragment. It turns your sacred messiness into something you start to resent. You scroll past laughter and start doubting your own joy. You see success and forget that you're only seeing the surface.

The algorithm doesn't just show you what you like — it learns what makes you feel *less than* and feeds you more of it. Because insecurity keeps you scrolling longer than happiness ever could. The critic inside swallows it all like junk food — quick, tempting, addictive. But instead of satisfaction, it leaves you hollow, hungry, and quietly mean to yourself. And when comparison tires you out, you crave something softer — a sense of belonging, even if it's borrowed. That's when gossip walks in, dressed as connection.

The Gossip Snack

It starts as background noise: a Slack thread, a coffee-room murmur, a group chat where colleagues air frustrations about management. You tell yourself you're just passing by — not contributing, just listening.

But gossip doesn't need your voice to enter your bloodstream. It seeps through the skin of attention. You lean in for "context," stay for "concern," and somewhere between the sighs and the side comments, your body starts reacting — a prickle in the chest, a shallow breath, a strange tension you can't name.

Negativity spreads quietly, like perfume you didn't mean to wear. By evening, you're carrying stories that aren't yours — someone else's anger, someone else's judgment, someone else's exhaustion — all echoing faintly in your mind. That's the trick of gossip: it masquerades as connection but feeds on separation. It bonds people through blame, momentarily soothing loneliness while deepening it. It leaves the heart salty, the conscience sticky, the mind heavier than before.

By nightfall, you feel drained, though nothing concrete happened to you. And when the room quiets, when everyone logs off, a familiar itch returns — the one that reaches for the phone "just for a minute."

The Binge Dessert

It's late. The day should be winding down, but your thumb keeps scrolling. Climate disasters. Celebrity scandals. Strangers on Twitter/X hurling insults in threads you'll never join.

You tell yourself it's "just online," but your body doesn't know the difference. The nervous system reacts as if the hurricane is ripping through your street, as if the shouting is happening in your living room. You promise yourself *just one more scroll.*

But while you do, the machine is learning. Every pause, every heartbeat, every hesitation is data. It studies what spikes your pulse, what holds your gaze, what keeps you from looking away. It learns that outrage and fear keep you engaged longer than joy ever could — that calm doesn't sell.

And so, it keeps feeding you storms. Not to inform you, but to keep you scrolling. You tell yourself you're catching up, but really, you're being caught. Each swipe is a small refusal to rest. Your eyes ache. Your breath thins. Inside, your nervous system hums like a fridge that never switches off.

You're not digesting content anymore — content is digesting you. The irony is cruel: you began the night seeking distraction, yet end it wired, lonely, and overfed on noise. What was meant to numb you has made you porous. You lie there, body buzzing, mind spinning, heart too full of borrowed storms to remember what calm feels like.

Each bite feels small. Just a nibble here, a scroll there. But by the end of the day, your mind feels bloated. Your chest tightens. Your mood sinks. Hope shrinks. Sleep fractures.

And just like junk food for the body, junk food for the mind is engineered to keep you coming back. Outrage, fear, and envy are flavors with long shelf lives. Algorithms know it. They serve it up like fast food at midnight — easy to grab, hard to resist, and always leaving you hungrier than before.

"Junk food for the mind feels urgent in the moment, but empties you in the end."

Reflection Prompt: Write down the top three "mental snacks" you consume most often. News? Negativity? Comparison? Gossip? Now ask yourself: how do I actually feel after consuming them – bloated, anxious, restless, or nourished?

Letting Go of Dark Chatter

Winter is already a season where biology tilts us toward heaviness. Serotonin — the neurotransmitter that steadies mood — runs lower. Melatonin — the hormone that signals night — lingers longer into the morning. The result? Your body is already leaning toward fatigue, your mind toward gloom.

Add to that a steady stream of dark chatter — outrage, arguments, breaking news, endless complaint threads — and it's like pouring buckets of ice water over an already shivering body. What could have been a manageable chill becomes a deep freeze.

The science is clear:

- Neuroplasticity: Every time you repeat a negative phrase ("this is miserable," "I can't take this anymore"), you are strengthening the neural pathway for despair. The groove deepens. The brain learns to default there.
- Doomscrolling and online arguments keep the stress hormone elevated long past the moment of exposure. Elevated cortisol erodes sleep, digestion, and immunity.
- The reticular activating system (RAS): This brain filter highlights whatever you prime it with. If your daily soundtrack is "the world is falling apart," your RAS will faithfully collect proof — every bleak headline, every failed plan, every dark sky.

But here's where winter offers a strange kind of gift: its bareness makes the clutter visible. The dark, the silence, the pause in pace — they give you a chance to notice. To hear what kind of words you are repeating. To ask: *Is this nourishment or noise?*

Letting go of dark chatter is not about ignoring the world. It is about choosing your diet of words with the same care you might choose your diet of food. Just as you shed clutter from closets in January, you can shed the clutter of thought and conversation. Just as you choose warming foods in winter to sustain the body, you can choose nourishing stories to sustain the mind.

"You are what you eat – but even more so,
you are what you repeat."

Reflection Prompt: For one week, write the three sentences you repeat most often – to yourself, or aloud. Are they heavy, draining, dark? Or do they offer even a flicker of light? Circle one sentence you want to retire, and one you want to repeat instead.

The Mind Diet Pyramid

If nutritionists created food pyramids to teach us balance, imagine a "mind diet pyramid" for winter:

- Base Layer – Daily Nourishment (eat freely): Uplifting music, inspiring books, comedy that makes you laugh aloud, meaningful conversations, time in nature, silence that restores.
- Middle Layer – Neutral Calories (moderation): Light entertainment, casual scrolling, non-inflammatory news, background chatter. Fine in moderation, but not the foundation.
- Top Layer – Junk Food (limit or avoid): Outrage politics, doomscrolling, toxic comment threads, comparison culture, gossip loops. They hijack your nervous system, leaving you drained and brittle.

When you see this pyramid clearly, you begin to make choices. Just as you swap fast food for something wholesome, you can swap an hour of scrolling for ten minutes of comedy or a page of poetry. Just as you meal-prep to stay nourished, you can "mind-prep" by curating playlists, podcasts, or books that lift you when the days are long.

Reflection Prompt: Sketch your personal mind pyramid. What's in your base layer? What's sneaking into your top layer too often? What one substitution can you make this week?

"Your body is shaped by food. Your spirit is shaped by input."

My Own Winter Companions

I know this truth personally.

One winter, back pain kept me housebound. Photography walks were impossible. Even simple tasks drained me. The walls closed in.

That's when new neighbors arrived — not in my building, but on my television. Sheldon, Penny, and Leonard from *The Big Bang Theory.* Kramer from *Seinfeld.* Their quirks, their banter, their laughter became my companions.

What began as background noise became medicine. Their humor softened the weight of pain. Their predictability steadied me when days felt uncertain.

Looking back, I see this story as part of the arc of acceptance and growth. In Chapter One, I had to accept limits. In Chapter Two, I learned that renewal could come quietly, like seeds beneath snow. And here, I discovered nourishment: not through food, but through laughter and connection, even fictional.

That winter taught me this: stories are not trivial. They are emotional nutrition. And sometimes, what you need most is not another headline, but a neighbor like Kramer or Sheldon bursting into your living room with ridiculous hair and a line that makes you laugh out loud.

> **Reflection Prompt:** What show, book, or character has carried you through a hard season? What did it feed you?

The Science of Input

Research confirms what we feel intuitively:

- Laughter lowers stress hormones.
- Endorphins act as natural pain relievers.
- Oxytocin, the bonding hormone, rises even when the bond is with fictional characters.
- A 2019 study in *Nature Human Behaviour* found that late-night screen use correlates with higher anxiety and disrupted sleep cycles.
- The American Academy of Sleep Medicine warns that scrolling before bed delays melatonin release and leads to fragmented sleep.

Your body reacts to what you consume — whether food or story. Doomscrolling floods your nervous system with stress. Comedy, warmth, and inspiration soothe it.

In winter, when biology already bends toward gloom, your **mental diet is not luxury. It is survival.**

Client Story – Breaking the Scroll Cycle

A client of mine, a young lawyer, confessed: *"I don't understand why I wake up anxious and go to bed restless. I'm exhausted, but my mind doesn't stop."*

We unpacked her habits. Morning: phone alarm, immediately scrolling headlines of conflict. Evening: scrolling again in bed, blue light blasting her eyes, anxiety and stress spiking with each negative thread.

I asked her to try one experiment: no scrolling in the first 20 minutes of the day, no scrolling in the 45 minutes before bed. Instead, she opened her curtains in the morning, breathing with the light, and ended the night with journaling.

By the second week, she told me: *"I didn't realize how much I was feeding my nervous system poison. Now my mornings feel calm, and my sleep feels deeper."*

Science backs her shift. Studies show that screen use at night delays melatonin release by up to 90 minutes, fragmenting sleep. In the morning, starting with negative news elevates puts the body into fight-or-flight before breakfast. Removing those two "scrolling snacks" changed her inner chemistry — her body could finally reset.

"What you reach for first and last rewrites your entire day."

Reflection Prompts: Integrating Nourishment

1. Mind Diet Audit

- List 5 inputs that nourish you.
- List 5 that drain you.
- Which dominates your days?

2. My Comfort List

- Write down 5 shows, books, or songs that always lift you.
- Place it somewhere visible for heavy days.

3. Digital Sunset Log

- Track how you feel after 3 nights screen-free. Note mood, energy, sleep.

4. Make your 7-Day Mind Diet Plan

- Morning: What will you feed your mind first?
- Midday: What breaks the stress spiral?
- Evening: What closes your day gently?
- Replace one draining snack daily with one nourishing input.

Closing Meditation – Nourishment Whole

Place one hand on your stomach, one on your chest. Breathe deeply.

Picture a warm bowl before you — soup, stew, or tea. Feel its heat radiating into your hands. As you inhale, imagine that warmth spreading through your body.

Now picture a story — a sitcom, a song, a book — filling your mind with lightness. Hear the laughter, the melody, the words.

You are nourished twice: body and mind.

Whisper to yourself: *"I nourish whole. Body. Mind. Spirit."*

> *"Nourishment is not just food on the plate, but the stories and silence we serve ourselves daily."*

Beyond Winter: The Larger Table

This chapter has focused on winter. But here is the truth: winter is only an example. Your table is set every day, in every season, in every inner winter of life.

When heartbreak arrives, when a job slips away, when burnout gnaws at your edges—the same question whispers: *what are you feeding yourself?*

Are you feeding outrage or inspiration? Complaint or gratitude? Noise or stillness?

Your inputs are not neutral. They are ingredients. They shape mood, memory, resilience, and even hope. A steady diet of dark chatter shrinks the world; a steady diet of light, laughter, and silence expands it.

The science confirms what wisdom has always known: what you repeat, you become. Every bite and every scroll is not just consumption—it is construction. You are building your nervous system, your inner atmosphere, your very sense of self.

And just as seeds beneath snow are quietly preparing for spring, the choices you make today—whether food, story, or silence—are shaping the self that will rise when your own winter passes.

The table is yours to set. Season after season. Moment after moment.

Reflection Prompt: Write down one nourishing input you will commit to daily–not just for winter, but for all seasons of your life.

"Your inputs become your identity. What you repeat becomes what you believe."

As we move into the next chapter, we will explore how breath, meditation, and visualization become daily nourishment of their own. If food fills the body and stories feed the mind, breath and meditation awaken the spirit. Together, they give you the resilience to not only endure winter, but to discover light within it.

CHAPTER THREE SUMMARY - NOURISHMENT: FEEDING BODY, MIND & SPIRIT

Key Insight

Softening resistance (Acceptance) and creating space (Openness) prepare the soil; what you feed it now helps determine what will grow. In winter – or any season of contraction – every input is either medicine or depletion. Food, stories, conversations, screens, self-talk: all shape your inner climate as much as the outer weather does. Conscious nourishment turns passive survival into quiet strengthening.

Core Metaphors

- Soil Under Frost: the inner ground you've prepared; what you feed it determines the harvest.
- Ancient Winter Tables: stews, myths, and candles as nervous-system medicine.
- Digital Diet: news, social feeds, and conversations as mental calories.
- Seed & Sunlight: a seed cracks but only grows when fed with light and warmth.

Rituals of Nourishment

- The Winter Mood Bowl - Once a week build a nutrient-rich bowl (omega-3s, complex carbs, colour) and pause before eating: "This is sunlight in another form."
- Steadying Sip Ritual - Make one warm drink a small ceremony instead of a rushed gulp.
- Mind Diet Audit - List five inputs that nourish you and five that drain you; swap one draining input for one nourishing input this week.

- Digital Sunset - No scrolling for 45 minutes before bed and 20 minutes after waking; replace with reading, night meditation, journaling, or simple soulful silence.
- Comfort List - Write down five shows, books, or songs that always lift you; keep it visible for heavy days.
- Story or Silence Reset - End your day with one intentional "feed": a chapter, a short comedy clip, or five minutes of quiet breathing.

Reflection Prompts

- What foods dominate my winter plate right now? Which leave me sluggish, and which leave me energised?
- What inputs dominate my "mental diet"? Which one can I replace with something nourishing this week?
- Sketch my personal "mind pyramid." What's in the base layer? What's sneaking into the top layer too often?
- Which story, book, or character has carried me through a hard season? What did it feed me?

Closing Meditation Mantra

"I nourish whole – body, mind, and spirit."

CHAPTER FOUR

Breathe and Believe

Harnessing the Power of Breath, Meditation, and Visualization to Find Winter Light

PART ONE - BREATHE

Prelude: Breath Made Visible

"Some things are so ordinary, we forget they are miracles until winter makes them visible."

Step outside on a January morning. The air is so sharp it stings. You brace yourself against the cold, shoulders rising, jaw tight. And then you exhale, and there it is — your breath made visible, swirling into the sky like smoke.

Most of the year, we forget it's there, this silent rhythm that sustains us. In winter, we are reminded: You are alive. You are still moving. Every cloud of breath is proof.

Anxiety has its own kind of winter. It freezes the body from the inside out. Shoulders rise, jaw tightens, and breath shrinks until it disappears

— hidden, shallow, unnoticed. You're still breathing, but only barely, like a stream under ice. Most of the year you can ignore it; in your personal "winters" of stress or loss you finally see it: the shallow chest, the skipped inhale, the nervous system braced to run.

That visibility is an invitation, not a condemnation. Just as frost outlines each branch, your anxious breath outlines where to begin. When you can see your breath, you can work with it. Each visible exhale becomes a reminder: "I'm alive. I can slow down. I can start here."

Breath became my medicine long before I called myself a coach. And every winter since has reminded me: breath is not just survival — it is light you can see. A rhythm you can return to when everything else feels unstable.

The Forgotten Gift

As children, we breathe from the belly — easy, deep, and soft. Watch a baby sleep and you'll see it: the rise and fall like waves on a calm ocean. But somewhere between growing up and showing up, we forget. Life demands. We brace. We compress. We become "chest breathers" — stuck in the upper lungs, always half-ready to flee.

I remember one particular winter when anxiety was my constant companion. I was in a corporate boardroom, heart pounding as a difficult meeting loomed. My chest tightened, my thoughts spiraled, and panic rose like a tide I couldn't control. I excused myself, stepped outside into the cold. The air slapped me awake. I focused on the only thing I could control — my breath. In. Out. Full belly breathing. Clouds forming, clouds dissolving. Slowly, my heart steadied. My hands stopped shaking. I walked back in, not transformed, but anchored.

Healing began — not through a book or a breakthrough, but through breath. Through the decision to inhale as if my life depended on it —

because it did. That is why this chapter is called **Breathe and Believe.** It's about reclaiming breath not only as survival but as your first act of self-trust.

This chapter is about reclaiming that light. About learning to breathe again - not just to survive, but to believe. To let each inhale anchor you in presence, and each exhale carry you closer to the life you want to create.

Part 1: Breath as Gateway
The Science of Breath: Biology Meets Spirit

Breath is the bridge. It is the only bodily function that is both automatic and under your control. You cannot will your heart to slow directly. You cannot demand your digestion to ease. But you can choose one slow inhale, one longer exhale — and in that choice, you influence the entire system.

Every inhale sends oxygen coursing through your blood, fueling every cell. Every exhale carries away carbon dioxide, releasing what no longer serves. But breath is more than chemistry. It is conversation with your nervous system.

- **The Nervous System:** Short, shallow breaths tell the body: *danger is near.* Long, deep breaths whisper: *safety is here.*
- **The Vagus Nerve:** This wandering nerve connects brain to gut, lungs, and heart. Slow exhalations stimulate it, activating the "rest and digest" system and calming stress.
- **Hormones:** Breath influences stress, serotonin (mood), and melatonin (sleep). Research shows that slow, deeper breathing shifts the body toward the parasympathetic ('rest-and-digest') state via vagal pathways and can modestly lower anxiety and blood pressure. A Stanford study found that five minutes a day of structured breathwork—especially an exhale-emphasized 'cyclic sigh'—improved mood and reduced stress more than mindfulness alone.

Ancient traditions knew this without MRI machines. This is where **Pranayama** enters the journey. The yogis have always known what modern science is only now proving: breath is the bridge between the body and the mind. "Prana" is life force. "Ayama" is expansion. Pranayama is not just about oxygen—it is about consciously directing the flow of energy through the body's channels, fueling every cell, every thought, every intention.

Across many traditions, breath practices were used in cold, dark seasons to steady nerves and focus attention. In Buddhist practice, the breath is the doorway to awakening. It is said that when you watch your breath, you are not just breathing—you are witnessing life itself, moment by moment. No past. No future. Just the inhale, just the exhale. As Thích Nhất Hạnh teaches, conscious breathing is a way of 'coming home'—arriving in the present moment. Each conscious breath is a return—back to the self, back to the present, back to the truth that you are more than your racing thoughts. Different cultures, same truth: breath is medicine.

Here's what I've learned in both practice and coaching: breath is not just a physiological hack. It is a spiritual rehearsal. When you breathe deeply, you are teaching your body to believe again in safety, in steadiness, in possibility.

Reflection Prompt: Recall a recent moment of stress. How did your breath feel – tight, shallow, rushed? Now recall a moment of calm. What was different? Write both down. Awareness is the first step to change.

Every calm begins with a single conscious breath. This one is easy to remember — and powerful enough to change your state within minutes.

I call it **a *breath of calm*** — a simple rhythm you can return to anywhere, at any time. Think of it as a quiet equation for balance: 4 + 2 = 6 — what you hold, you release; what you give attention to, you free.

How to Practice

1. Inhale through the nose for *4 counts* — slow and steady, filling belly, ribs, and chest.
2. Hold for *2 counts* — not straining, simply pausing at the threshold between inhale and exhale.
3. Exhale through the mouth for *6 counts* — longer, slower, letting tension pour out.
4. Repeat this rhythm 3–5 times, or until you feel your breath steady and your mind begin to gather.

Already, your nervous system starts to downshift; your scattered energy begins to return home.

This breath is a reminder: meditation doesn't wait for stillness — it begins the moment you choose to breathe with awareness.

Notice: When the exhale lengthens, the body whispers safety back to the mind — and calm becomes something you can feel, not just chase.

Diaphragmatic Breathing – The Breaths of Calm

If the **4-2-6** breath is a doorway, diaphragmatic breathing is the **resting bench inside**. It's the simplest way to return to calm when winter feels heavy, or life feels crowded.

Place one hand on your belly and one on your chest. Inhale so the **belly rises first**, then the chest. Exhale slowly, belly falling. That's it. This is your anchor.

I often teach clients to use this as a simple reset:

- Between meetings or difficult conversations
- Before sleep
- When the inner critic starts shouting

Even two or three rounds can change your chemistry. This is not just breathwork; it's a quiet declaration: *I am slowing down. I am present here, not racing ahead.*

How to Practice

1. Sit or lie comfortably. Place one hand on your belly, one on your chest.
2. Inhale gently through the nose, letting the belly rise first, then the chest.
3. Exhale slowly through the mouth, belly falling.
4. As you breathe, silently repeat the mantra:
   "I am breathing in calm. I am breathing out stress."
5. Continue for 2–5 rounds, or longer if it feels good.

Dirga Pranayama – The Full Winter Breath

If diaphragmatic breathing is the bench where you pause, **Dirga Pranayama** — the yogic three-part breath — is the quiet walk through the full house of your lungs.

Begin softly. **Inhale** in three gentle waves:

- **Belly:** the base expands first, loosening like earth preparing for roots.
- **Ribs:** the middle widens, branches stretching toward light.
- **Chest:** the crown lifts last, as if sunlight is entering through the collarbones.

Then **exhale** in the same order — chest, ribs, belly — a tide flowing back to shore. Let the breath roll like water: even, continuous, unhurried.

After a few minutes, the motion becomes seamless — no beginning, no end. Just breath arriving and departing, cleansing and steady, like the tide's eternal rhythm against the winter shore.

Notice: As the wave of breath rises and falls, your awareness begins to rest in the space between — still, weightless, alive.

Why do these breathing techniques work?

- **Biology:** Activates the vagus nerve and parasympathetic system, lowering heart rate and calming stress hormones.
- **Psychology:** Gives your mind a simple focal point (breath + mantra), interrupting spirals of thought.
- **Spirit:** Becomes a moment of self-kindness, not a task to complete.

Note for Readers: You don't need to do them all. Choose one practice a day. Let it be your anchor. Depth comes from consistency, not quantity. These breathing and meditation practices are for general well-being and are **not** medical care. If you have a respiratory, cardiovascular, or psychiatric condition, are pregnant, or feel dizzy, light-headed, or short of breath, **stop and return to natural breathing**. Avoid long breath holds, hyperventilation, or practicing while driving or in water. Consult a qualified clinician if unsure.

From Arrival to Light

Once you learn to arrive in breath — through the 4-2-6 rhythm, belly breathing, or pranayama — you begin the journey from survival to steadiness, from steadiness to light.

Breath is the body's oldest compass. It gathers what the mind scatters and brings you home to the present. And now, science echoes what ancient wisdom has long taught: slow, rhythmic breathing can calm the brain's fear centers within minutes. Studies show that even a few rounds of deep diaphragmatic breathing can shift the body out of the stress-driven "fight or flight" mode and into the parasympathetic state — the body's natural rhythm of rest, repair, and safety.

In other words, a few mindful breaths can literally rewire your inner weather. The storms don't vanish — but your ground becomes steadier.

This is where true presence begins: when the breath is calm, the mind clears; when the mind clears, light returns. Each breath becomes a doorway — first to awareness, then to peace.

But breath is only the beginning. Once you can inhale light and exhale fear, once you can fan your own flame — what comes next is attention. Breath roots you, but meditation lets you look, without flinching, at what is within- the northern light that's been waiting for you all along.

PART 2: BELIEVE

Meditation – Attention, Not Escape

For years, I knew *how* to meditate — I had studied the techniques, understood the breath ratios, even taught others the theory of stillness. And yet, I resisted the practice itself. My mind was too loud, too restless, too full of unfinished thoughts.

I kept trying to *do* meditation — to control the chaos, to force silence — and every time the mind refused to obey, I told myself, *"This isn't for me."*

Then came my first winter in Toronto. The city was new, unfamiliar. The streets moved slower under the weight of fresh snow, and a strange hush settled over everything. One evening, I stood by the window, watching the flakes fall under a dim streetlight. Cars crawled by. Breath fogged the glass. Time itself seemed to soften.

My camera sat beside me, but for once, I didn't reach for it. I wasn't trying to capture the moment — I was letting it capture me. Each flake landed and vanished — ordinary, fleeting, complete.

And in that quiet, I finally understood: meditation isn't about escape. It isn't the absence of thought — it's the presence of awareness. It's the gentle art of noticing life as it unfolds, without rushing to change it.

The snow kept falling, and for the first time in a long while, I simply let it.

Meditation is not concentration. Concentration narrows; meditation opens. It doesn't demand that you stop thinking — only that you start listening. Your mind will wander — that's its nature. The practice is not in preventing the drift, but in the tender act of returning. No shame. No judgment. Just return.

Each time you come back, you're not failing at meditation — you're finding your way home.

"Meditation is not control.
It is surrender to presence."

The DOs and DON'Ts of Meditation

Think of these not as rules, but as gentle guardrails—reminders that keep meditation from becoming another self-punishing task.

The DOs

- **Do begin with acceptance.**
Before you close your eyes, accept everything exactly as it is — the hum of the fridge, the traffic outside, the uneven temperature of the room. Don't wait for perfect silence or ideal conditions. The moment you stop

arguing with your surroundings, the mind loses one of its oldest excuses: *"It's too noisy, too warm, too cold."* Meditation begins where resistance ends.

- **Do choose your place and return to it.**
Be consistent in where you sit. It doesn't have to be elaborate — a chair by the window, a mat in a quiet corner, even a spot on the floor by your bed. With repetition, that space absorbs your stillness. Over time, it becomes your **Calm Corner**— a pocket of peace you've built yourself, breath by breath.

- **Do let the process unfold naturally.**
Approach meditation as an invitation, not an assignment. Let your practice grow the way snow gathers — gently, layer by layer, without hurry.

- **Do sit with kindness.**
Choose a posture that's steady but comfortable. Let your body feel rooted yet soft. Small movements to adjust are fine; comfort supports focus.

- **Do return to your breath.**
When thoughts arise (and they will), notice them kindly, then guide your attention back to the rhythm of your breathing. Each return is an act of grace, not failure.

- **Do end with a smile.**
Before you finish, take one more slow breath, soften your face, and offer yourself a small smile. This anchors your practice in warmth and gratitude.

- **Do carry the practice into your day.**
Pause before moving on. Notice what's shifted — a sense of calm, clarity, or steadiness — and take that feeling with you. Let the end of your meditation be a beginning, not a cut-off point.

- **Do honour rest.**
Sleep and stillness are partners. Let meditation support, not replace, your natural rhythms of rest.

The DON'Ts

- **Don't expect a blank mind.**
The mind is a sky, not a whiteboard. Clouds drift through — let them.

- **Don't force stillness.**
Hold your posture like a tree that bends, stable yet flexible. Forcing stillness only breeds tension.

- **Don't chase "perfect" sessions.**
Meditation is not a performance. Some days will feel peaceful, others restless. Both are practice.

- **Don't treat meditation as escape.**
It won't erase pain, but it will teach you to hold it gently — without drowning in it.

- **Don't rush into "dumpster diving."**
After meditating, resist the pull to grab your phone, check the news, or scroll social media. It's like applying a beautiful perfume and then stepping into a dumpster — the sharp contrast can undo the calm you've created. Give yourself a soft landing.

- **Don't judge your progress harshly.**
Each breath, each return to presence, is progress — especially on difficult days. The goal is not perfection, but consistency, kindness, and presence.

Meditation deepens not by effort but by return — showing up to the same breath, the same corner, the same imperfect conditions, until that space begins to hold you in return.

Why Meditation Works

Meditation is not philosophy alone; it reshapes you on three levels.

- **Biology:** Slow breathing and steady attention activate the parasympathetic nervous system, slowing heart rate, and restoring balance.
- **Psychology:** Meditation builds metacognition — the ability to notice thoughts without being consumed by them. You step out of the spiral and into awareness.
- **Spirit:** Meditation reconnects you with presence — the only place life actually happens. In presence, even winter's silence becomes sacred.

My 15+ Years of Practice

I didn't come to meditation through ease; I came through resistance — through years of restlessness, anxiety, and trying to control what couldn't be controlled. But over time, the practice found its way into my life again and again — in boardrooms and monasteries, in pain and in stillness.

Over the last fifteen years, through winters of anxiety, back pain, career upheaval, and the quiet demands of everyday life, I've sat with monks in India and walked alone through snowfields in Canada. I've guided clients who once said, *"I can't meditate,"* into moments of deep connection. I've watched corporate leaders pause with three slow breaths before a meeting and find more clarity than hours of analysis ever gave them.

Through all of it, I've learned one truth: meditation is not a technique — it's a relationship. A way of being with what is, rather than escaping it.

From these experiences, certain practices have stayed with me — meditations that anchor in light, in body, in silence. They are not techniques on a menu, they are living companions for every season. A lineage I carry — and offer to you — because they've held me through my hardest winters and led me, again and again, back to the still center that waits beneath every storm.

That, I've come to understand, is **yoga** in its truest sense — not movement or posture, but *union*: the meeting of you with your real self, your soul, your **Ātman**. It is the return to what has always been steady beneath all change — the part of you untouched by fear, chaos, or circumstance.

For this book, I've chosen meditations that bring you closest to that steadiness — practices that work best in the colder, quieter months when life slows and reflection deepens. These are tools for both kinds of winters — the ones outside your window, and the ones that arrive within. Each one is a lantern for the dark, a way of finding warmth when the world feels frozen.

Because the goal was never to escape the winter — it was to remember the light that lives within it.

A Gentle Breath Before the Practices

Before beginning any meditation, take a few moments to arrive and pause through breath. Choose whichever pattern feels most natural — the **4-2-6 breath**, **diaphragmatic breathing**, or simply what your body asks for today.

If you'd like a guide, try this:

- **Inhale** deeply for a count of **4**, filling belly, ribs, and chest.
- **Hold** gently for a count of **2**, letting the breath settle — not straining, just pausing.
- **Exhale** slowly for a count of **6**, releasing resistance with each breath out.

Repeat this rhythm for two or three rounds. Feel how each cycle softens the edges of thought, loosens the shoulders, and prepares the body to receive meditation — like loosening the soil before planting seeds.

Even a single round creates space. A few rounds open the inner doorway, letting calm begin before stillness even arrives.

Breath is the bridge between doing and being — cross it slowly.

It is from this breath — this pause — that my own signature practices were born. Some came on grey Toronto mornings when the sun hid for weeks, yet I still felt its presence.

The most enduring one for me, and for many of my clients, is what I call the **Third Eye Sun Meditation**. It begins with breath, but it is fueled by visualization and belief — a way of carrying the light inside, even on the darkest winter day.

• The Third Eye Sun Meditation – Carrying Light Within

There were Toronto mornings when the sky was iron-grey for days on end. No sunrise, no golden shaft breaking through blinds — only a heaviness that seemed to seep into the bones. On one of those mornings, I sat by my window and decided: if the sun would not come to me, I would go to it.

I closed my eyes, placed one hand on my chest and one on my belly, and breathed slowly. On each inhale, I imagined light pouring through my forehead, through the space yogic traditions call the **third eye**. At first, it felt forced. I thought: *how can I drink light that isn't there?* But breath after breath, something shifted. My body began to warm. My mind softened. Even on a day when the outside sky withheld its brightness, my inner sky glowed.

That was the birth of the practice I now call the **Third Eye Sun Meditation**. It is both biological and spiritual: a way of giving the nervous system what it craves — light, serotonin, rhythm — while giving the spirit what it longs for — connection, radiance, a reminder that we are not in darkness alone.

How to Practice
Step One: Anchor in Breath
Start with your choice of breathing technique.

Step Two: Face the Sun (or Imagine It)

- If the sun is shining, sit or stand near a window and face the light.
- If the day is cloudy, dim, or dark, close your eyes and **visualize the sun** — a golden sphere above you, infinite in energy, generous in warmth.

Step Three: Draw Light In

- Close your eyes.
- Inhale for a count of 4 and imagine sunlight entering through the space between your eyebrows — the **third eye chakra (located between your eyebrows)**, associated with clarity and insight.
- Hold for a count of 2, letting the light gather there.
- Exhale for a count of 6, letting the light spill through your body — head, throat, chest, belly, legs, feet.
- Repeat 7–10 times.

Step Four: Expand to Chakras *(Optional, for deeper practice)*

As you continue, allow the light to travel further:

- From the third eye (Ajna), it floods the crown (Sahasrara) with wisdom.
- Down through the throat (Vishuddha), clearing communication.
- Into the heart (Anahata), warming compassion.
- Into the belly (Manipura), igniting confidence.
- Into the root (Muladhara), grounding you with strength.

On cloudy days, this visualization becomes even more powerful — because you are reminding your body that light is not only external. It is also internal.

Why It Works

- **Science of Light:** Sunlight boosts serotonin, stabilizing mood and energy. Even visualization of light can shift brain chemistry by activating similar neural pathways.
- **Chakra Tradition:** Yogic philosophy holds that the third eye is the seat of inner vision. When you imagine light flowing through it, you are practicing clarity and awakening insight.

- **Neuroscience of Imagery:** The brain often responds to imagined stimuli as if they were real. Visualizing light warms mood and body, even in the absence of actual sunlight.
- **Personal Experience:** Clients who practiced this daily reported not just calmer mornings, but a stronger sense of "inner radiance." One told me: *"Even on stormy days, I no longer wait for the sun. I carry it."*

Client Story – Carrying the Sun

A client of mine, working through grief after losing a parent, felt mornings were unbearable. "The sky feels like it's pressing me down," she said. I invited her to try this practice — not once, but daily for three weeks.

At first, she resisted: *"It feels fake. The sun isn't here."* But gradually, she wrote in her journal: *"I feel a glow behind my eyes, even when it rains."*

By the third week, she said: *"I don't wait for light to arrive anymore. I create it."* That sentence was her turning point. Winter hadn't changed. But she had.

Reflection Prompt: After practicing the Third Eye Sun Meditation, write in your journal:

- *What did the light feel like inside me?*
- *Where in my body did it travel?*
- *What shifted in my mood after seven breaths of sunlight?*

*"When the sun hides,
become the one who carries it."*

Supporting Meditations – Branches of the Same Tree

Your breath is the root, the Sun Meditation is the trunk, and these supporting meditations are the branches. Each carries light differently — some in the body, some in silence — but all flow from the same source: presence.

• Body Scan for Sleep – Letting Go Like Snow

This practice is drawn from the ancient tradition of **Yoga Nidra** ("yogic sleep"), a form of guided relaxation designed to take you to the edge between wakefulness and rest. In classical texts it was used to restore the nervous system and prepare the mind for deeper states of meditation. Here, we adapt it in a simple, modern way to help you shift from alert to ease at night.

Sleep is one of your most essential allies in meditation. When rest feels elusive, a gentle body scan can help your system downshift naturally.

A client once confessed: *"I dread night. It's when the noise in my head gets loudest."* Sleep for her was a battlefield.

I guided her through a body scan: toes, calves, thighs, belly, chest, jaw. With each breath she imagined snow falling gently, covering and softening tension. Night after night, she practiced. Within weeks, she told me: *"I no longer fear sleep. It feels like surrender, not battle."*

This simple ritual is meditation's quiet partner—an act of letting go that prepares your mind and body for the deep restoration they deserve.

How to Practice

Welcome and Settling
Close your eyes. Place one hand on your chest, one on your belly. Feel the mattress supporting you, the pillow cradling your head, the blanket softly hugging your body. Notice where you make contact with the bed — shoulders, hips, heels. Let your jaw loosen.

Take three slow diaphragmatic breaths. Inhale for a count of four. Hold for a count of two. Exhale for a count of 7 or 8 (longer the better). With each exhale, imagine sinking a little deeper into the mattress.

Body Scan

Now bring your attention to your toes.
Breathe in gently, and as you exhale,
imagine a soft wave of calm moving through them —
light, soothing, melting away tension.
Silently whisper, "I release you."
Move your awareness to your feet and ankles.
Inhale. Exhale. "I release you."
Up to your calves… warmth and ease flowing in.
Your thighs and hips… tightness dissolving,
the surface beneath you holding you completely.
Your belly… feel the rise and fall under your hand.
Breathe in rest,
breathe out thoughts.
Your chest… notice each breath softening your heartbeat.
Your shoulders and arms… let go of the weight you've been carrying.
Your hands… fingers uncurl, palms soften.
Your neck and jaw… tension melting away with every exhale.
Your eyes and scalp… light, calm, and free.
Whisper again, "I release you."
If at any point thoughts intrude,
simply notice them, and gently return
your awareness to the last body part you remember.

Closing

Now sense your whole body at once — from toes to crown — relaxed and whole. Whisper softly:

"With every breath, I'm sinking deeper into the mattress… into the pillow… breathing in calm… breathing out thoughts."

Take one more slow breath.
Soften your face.
Offer yourself a small smile.
Allow yourself to drift into rest.

Why it Works

- **Biology:** Activates the parasympathetic nervous system.
- **Psychology:** Shifts focus from racing thoughts to grounded body awareness.
- **Spirit:** Sleep becomes less about shutting down and more about laying down what you've carried.

> **Reflection Prompt:** Write: *What part of my body felt most resistant? What part softened the most?*

*"Sleep is not surrender.
It is the soul's rehearsal for peace."*

• Silent Sitting – Presence Without Striving

On one of my trips to Banff National Park in Canada, I raised my camera to capture snow — but lowered it again. For twenty minutes I simply sat and watched. No lens, no agenda. Just silence falling in white layers.

That moment taught me something: meditation isn't always posture, mantra, or technique. Sometimes it's presence so complete that the ordinary turns holy.

How to Practice

- Step outside or look out a window on a snowy day. If you live elsewhere, simply imagine snow or another quiet natural scene — rain, leaves falling, waves rolling in.

- Sit or stand still. Allow your body to settle without trying to "get it right."
- Watch or imagine. Let each flake, drop, leaf, or moment of stillness be your mantra. No words needed — just awareness.
- When your mind wanders, gently return to the falling, drifting, or flowing.

Why It Works

- Biology: Research on attention restoration shows that simply watching nature softens mental fatigue and restores clarity.
- Psychology: Observing without striving teaches non-attachment — the art of seeing without grasping.
- Spirit: Snow (or any quiet natural movement) reminds us that silence is not empty; it is full of presence.

> **Reflection Prompt:** *Write: What did I hear or feel in the silence that I usually miss?*

"Silence is not absence.
It is presence widened."

How These Meditations Flow Together

- **Breath** is the entryway: slowing the body, steadying the mind.
- **Third Eye Sun** gives direction: carrying inner light when outer light fails.
- **Body Scan** provides rest: teaching surrender when the day resists.
- **Silent Snow** offers stillness: reminding you that presence alone is enough.

Together, they are not separate practices, but a **circle of winter meditation**. Light, rest, silence — each one prepares you for the next chapter on visualization, where the presence you've cultivated turns into direction for growth.

Remember: Calm isn't the absence of challenge — it's the rhythm you hold within it.

If breath is fuel and meditation is presence, visualization is direction. It is where you stop only noticing and begin imagining. It is the moment you tell your inner world: *this is where I want to grow.*

Visualization – Planting Seeds Beneath Snow

Prelude: From Stillness to Direction

Breath steadies the nervous system. Meditation anchors presence. But stillness alone isn't enough. Once you've learned to sit in the quiet, a new question rises: *Where do I want this quiet to lead me?*

That is the doorway to visualization.

Meditation notices what is. Visualization rehearses what can be. Together, they complete the circle. Breath fuels. Meditation grounds. Visualization directs.

The Science of Seeing Ahead

Neuroscience confirms what sages intuited: the brain runs simulations before it runs actions. Imagine yourself lifting a cup and motor neurons fire. Imagine yourself walking into a room with calm, and your nervous system begins to practice it. This is called neuroplasticity — the brain wiring new pathways from imagined rehearsal.

Your brain is already a rehearsal machine. Before you pick up a glass, your motor cortex runs a simulation of the movement. Before a tough conversation, you imagine how it might unfold. Visualization takes this natural process and focuses it with purpose.

- Neural pathways: Research at the Cleveland Clinic found that participants who only visualized lifting weights increased muscle strength by 13 percent. Their brains activated motor neurons almost as if the exercise had really happened.
- The nervous system: The body doesn't always distinguish vividly imagined experiences from real ones. Imagine standing on stage and your heart may race. Imagine roots grounding you, and your breath begins to steady.
- Mood regulation: In winter, when light and color are scarce, imagery becomes an internal supplement. Brain scans show imagining bright light can activate parts of the visual cortex similar to real sunlight.
- Visualization is not daydreaming. It is neuroplasticity at work—retraining your brain to expect growth, resilience, and renewal.
- Athletes visualize before performing. Muscles prime as if already moving.
- Musicians rehearse mentally; brain scans show nearly identical activity to actual playing.
- Patients visualizing healing often show measurable improvement in recovery and mood.

Winter offers a metaphor here: beneath the snow and ice, seeds germinate unseen. Visualization is planting those seeds in the soil of your nervous system.

Why Winter Needs Visualization Most

Winter starves the senses – whether real or metaphorical. Grey skies dim the light. Trees stand bare. Our bodies instinctively wait for cues of renewal — warmth on skin, color in fields, blossoms in sight. But sometimes those cues don't come for months.

Visualization gives you those cues from within. It lets your nervous system rehearse safety, strength, and joy, even when the outside world offers none.

When the landscape is stripped, imagination becomes a lantern like the third eye sun meditation

Neuroscience shows that mental imagery activates many of the same pathways as lived experience. When you picture yourself standing strong, your nervous system begins to learn strength. When you imagine light pouring into your chest, serotonin shifts upward, mood steadies.

And spiritually, visualization is faith in action. A seed beneath snow is not visible, but it is real. You don't pretend it will sprout — you trust it. You don't wish for the sun — you breathe it in, even on cloudy days.

Visualization is where science meets surrender: the brain rehearses, but the soul believes.

Entering the Practices

These pages are more than exercises; they're doorways. Each Calm Mind practice you're about to meet is a signature meditation developed through years of working with clients and my own seasons of change. They blend breath, visualization, and gentle self-inquiry to help you shift from tension to steadiness, from heaviness to light.

You don't have to "get them right." You don't have to master posture, empty your mind, or achieve instant peace. These are living practices — ways of remembering what's already within you. Some will speak to you immediately, others you may return to later.

Most begin with the Breaths of Calm to settle your nervous system, then guide you inward through images, sensations, and simple mantras. In "Happy Place" you discover a portable sanctuary. In "Seed Visualization" you plant new beginnings. In "Future-Self Walk" you borrow wisdom from the you who has already walked this path. In "Smile Visualization" you awaken warmth on the hardest days.

Think of these not as lessons, but as companions. They're invitations to slow down, to feel, to remember:

"When you can't go out, you can go in — and find the paradise within."

Use them when mornings feel heavy, evenings feel crowded, or life feels uncertain. Use them at your desk, on a bus, or before sleep. Let them meet you where you are, and trust that each small return to the breath is progress.

Happy Place – A Signature Calm Mind Meditation

This is one of my most powerful Calm Mind practices. It shows how quickly meditation and visualization can shift your inner state. We begin with the Breaths of Calm, then travel inward to a place where safety, ease and joy already live.

When you can't go out, you can go in — and discover your own paradise. Your Happy Place is a portable sanctuary you can visit anytime to restore balance and light.

How to Practice

- **Settle in.** Sit or lie comfortably. Close your eyes. Place one hand on your belly, one on your chest.
- **Begin with the Breaths of Calm (4-2-6).** Inhale gently for a count of 4, hold for 2, exhale for 6. Or diaphragmic breath. Do three rounds. Feel your body softening with each breath (Reminder – no straining).
- **Step into your Happy Place.** Imagine you are at the beach (or any place you love). Engage all your senses:
  - **Sight:** Notice the colour of the sky, the way light dances on the water, the shape of the horizon.
  - **Sound:** Hear the gentle crash of waves, distant seabirds, your own slow breathing.
  - **Touch:** Feel the sand between your toes, the sea breeze on your skin, the warmth of sunlight.

   - **Smell:** Breathe in the salty air or the scent of pine, flowers, or rain if your place is different.
   - **Taste:** Imagine the taste of cool water, fresh air, or a favourite drink you'd have there.
- **Optional:** Bring in your inner guide. Feel a calm, reassuring presence beside you — perhaps me, or someone who makes you feel safe. Hear the quiet reminder: "You are safe. You are already whole."
- **Anchor with a mantra.** Silently repeat: **"I am breathing in calm. I am breathing out stress."**
- **Stay for a few breaths.** Let the scene become more vivid with each inhale, more peaceful with each exhale. When your mind wanders, gently return to the breath and the sensory details of your Happy Place.
- **Close gently.** Before you open your eyes with a smile, take one more slow breath and imagine carrying a small piece of this place back into your day.

Why It Works

- **Biology:** Multi-sensory imagery activates the parasympathetic system, lowering heart rate and easing muscle tension.
- **Psychology:** Guided visualization helps your brain rehearse calm and safety, strengthening new pathways for resilience.
- **Spirit:** Your Happy Place becomes a portable sanctuary — a reminder that peace is always one breath and one image away.

> **Reflection Prompt:** *Write: Which senses felt easiest to engage? Which detail from my Happy Place felt most soothing?*

"When you can't go out, you can go in – and feel the paradise within."

Seed Visualization – Planting the Future

Breath First:
Place a hand on your belly. Inhale 4, hold 2, exhale 6. Repeat seven times, exhaling each time with the whisper: *I release what is done.*

Meditation:
Rest your attention on your open palm. Place a grain of rice or pebble there. Whisper: *This is possibility.*

Visualization:
Picture a seed beneath the snow. Still. Resting. Waiting. See it swell, crack, and send down roots. Imagine a pale shoot curling upward, not rushing, but persistent. Each day you return, keep it warm with your presence. You water it with small daily acts.

Client Reflection:
One client whispered, "I want to change careers, but I'm terrified." Instead of diving into résumés, we began with seeds. He pictured his new life as a seed each night. By March, he had a prototype. By May, a paying client. "I planted it here first," he said, touching his chest.

> **Reflection Prompt:** Name your seed. Write the one act you will take tomorrow to water it.

Future-Self Walk – Borrowing Wisdom

As I have mentioned earlier in the book, in Tromso, Norway, winter isn't endured; it's embraced. Lanterns glow on streets where the sun disappears for months. Cafés hum with laughter and candlelight. People don't wait for warmth — they *create* it. They anticipate the dark season with preparation, not fear.

This meditation borrows that same wisdom. It invites you to meet your **future self** — the version of you who has already lived through this winter, inner or outer, with steadiness and grace.

Close your eyes and picture a snow-covered path. You're walking through it slowly, breath visible in the crisp air.

Ahead, a faint figure approaches. Look closer — it's you, months from now. Notice how your future self moves: shoulders relaxed, steps unhurried, eyes bright with calm and quiet confidence.

There's a gentle warmth in their smile — the kind that comes from trust, not perfection. Their presence feels light, open, content — not untouched by challenge, but unshaken by it. There's a soft joy about them, a peace that doesn't need to announce itself.

Stand face-to-face for a moment.

Feel what it's like to be in your future self's company — to meet the version of **you** who has learned to breathe through storms and still find wonder in the snow. As you linger here, notice the connection forming — the boundary between "you" and "them" beginning to blur. This calm, this steadiness, this quiet joy — it's already yours.

What does your future self want you to know?

Which qualities — patience, ease, optimism, or trust — do you sense growing within yourself even now?

Sometimes, this visualization brings a symbol.

A compass may appear — reminding you to stay aligned with your true north.

A cup may form in your hands — whispering, *keep filling and refilling; don't pour from emptiness.*

A metronome might emerge — a gentle rhythm saying, *Pace yourself; don't sprint and collapse.*

These are not just metaphors — they are instructions. Each one carries a quiet code for how to move through your present moment.

Your future self is not far away — it is already whispering through your calmest moments, waiting for you to listen.

> **Reflection Prompt:** Describe the gift your future self gave you. What message or feeling came with it? What does it teach you about how to walk forward through this season – both in the world and within yourself?

The Science of Future-Self Visualization

Neuroscience now confirms what ancient wisdom has long known: the brain doesn't fully distinguish between imagination and lived experience. When you vividly picture your **future self** thriving, your neural pathways encode that image as a likely reality.

Psychologists call this *episodic future thinking* — the ability to mentally rehearse the traits you want to strengthen. By visualizing yourself steady, peaceful, and joyful, you train your mind to make present choices aligned with that future state.

You're not escaping reality — you're *preparing* for it. Each time you meet your future self in calm, you bring a little of their wisdom — and their light — back into today.

Smile Visualization – Breathing Light into Low Days when you have less time

This is another signature Calm Mind practice developed by me. It's designed for the days when heaviness feels glued to your chest and you need a gentle way back to yourself. Even an imagined smile can soften the weight.

In this meditation, you combine slow breathing, a hand on the heart, and a happy memory to awaken your body's natural calm. Instead of forcing positivity, you invite warmth and light from the inside out — a quiet, practical way to remind yourself that joy still lives within you.

How to Practice

- **Find a quiet spot.** Sit or lie comfortably. Place one hand on your heart. Let the other rest wherever it feels natural.
- **Begin with three slow diaphragmatic breaths.** Inhale for a count of four, hold for two, exhale for six. With each exhale, feel your hand warming your heart.
- **Visualize a moment of joy.** Recall a simple, happy memory — a laugh with a friend, sunlight on your face, the smell of fresh coffee. See it as clearly as you can.
- **Imagine yourself smiling in that moment.** Picture your own face softening, eyes brightening, chest expanding.
- **Let the smile spread.** As you breathe, imagine that smile moving from your face through your chest, shoulders, arms, belly, and legs — a quiet warmth filling your whole body.
- **Anchor with a mantra.** Silently repeat: **"I am breathing in calm. I am breathing out heaviness."** Or **"I am breathing in calm. I am breathing out stress."**
- **Stay for a few breaths.** When your mind wanders, gently return to your hand on your heart and your inner smile.

Why It Works

- **Biology:** Studies suggest that even an imagined smile triggers a small release of endorphins and helps regulate heart rhythm.
- **Psychology:** Pairing breath with positive memory rewires the brain's stress loops and reminds you of your capacity for joy.
- **Spirit:** The smile becomes a beacon — not a mask — a way of remembering your own light on dark days.

Reflection Prompt: *Write: Which memory brought the easiest smile today? How did my body feel after the practice?*

"A smile is not a performance. It's a doorway back to your own light."

Closing Reflection – From Seeing to Speaking

Visualization is rehearsal. Each root you imagine, each seed you tend in silence, each aurora you let dance inside your chest — these are not fantasies. They are rehearsals of safety, possibility, and awe. Your body doesn't always wait for proof from the outside world; it begins to believe what you show it within.

But seeing alone is not the whole practice. What is seen must be spoken. Breath carries life, meditation anchors attention, visualization directs energy — and affirmations seal it with words.

If roots anchor you, affirmations will remind you: *I am being rooted.* If seeds grow within you, affirmations will say: *I am growing each day.* If lights shimmer inside your chest, affirmations will echo, *I am carrying light into this night.*

This is the flow:

breath steadies → meditation clears → visualization plants → affirmations speak life into the planted seed.

Affirmations are those drops — daily, deliberate, spoken aloud. In the next chapter, we will give voice to the visions you've planted.

CHAPTER FOUR SUMMARY - BREATHE & BELIEVE: HARNESSING THE POWER OF BREATH, MEDITATION & VISUALIZATION TO FIND WINTER LIGHT

Key Insight

Breath is your built-in bridge between body and mind – the one rhythm you can consciously influence. In winter, when everything slows and anxiety tightens the chest, visible breath becomes a cue: "I'm alive. I can start here." Slow, deliberate breathing steadies the nervous system; meditation turns that steadiness into presence; visualization turns presence into direction. Together, they let you carry light within when the outer world feels dark.

Core Metaphors

- Breath Made Visible: Winter frost reveals the miracle you usually overlook.
- Stream Under Ice: Shallow, anxious breathing as hidden life waiting to thaw.
- Seeds Beneath Snow: Visualization as planting possibility before it's visible.
- Third-Eye Sun: Becoming the one who carries the light when the sun hides.

Rituals of Breath, Meditation & Visualization

- 4-2-6 Breath – Arriving (4 + 2 = 6 for ease)
  Inhale for 4 counts, hold for 2, exhale for 6. Repeat 3–5 cycles to downshift the nervous system and cue calm.
- Diaphragmatic / Dirga Breathing – Winter Pauses
  Hand on belly, hand on chest; breathe from base to ribs to chest, then exhale slowly. Feel the breath lengthen and ground you.

- Third-Eye Sun Meditation – Carrying Light Within
  After anchoring in breath, visualize sunlight entering the space between your brows, travelling through your inner centers, filling you with radiance even on grey days.
- Body Scan for Sleep – Letting Go Like Snow
  Move attention from toes upward, whispering "I release you" at each point to invite rest.
- Silent Sitting with Snow – Presence Without Striving
  Sit in stillness (or imagine snowfall) and observe without effort. Each return to awareness is part of the practice.
- Future-Self Walk – Borrowing Wisdom
  Visualize meeting your future self who has already lived this winter well; notice a symbolic "gift" or phrase they offer as guidance.
- Smile Meditation – Remembered Joy
  Combine slow breathing, a hand on the heart, and a warm memory to awaken your body's natural calm.

Reflection Prompts:

- Recall a recent moment of stress. How did your breath feel? Recall a moment of calm. What was different?
- After your Third-Eye Sun meditation: What did the light feel like inside you? Where did it travel?
- Sketch your visualization journey. Which image felt most real or healing?
- Write one present-tense affirmation after each visualization to begin turning imagery into belief.

Closing Meditation Mantra

"When the sun hides, become the one who carries it."

CHAPTER FIVE

Words We Are Breathing: The Power of Affirmations

Affirmations are not slogans.
They're living sentences you breathe until the heart remembers.

Prelude: The Weather Inside Our Words

I step outside into a January morning, my breath making small ghosts in the air. In Chapter Four we learned to anchor with breath—inhale, hold, exhale—letting the body remember safety. Here, we let words ride that breath so the sentences being repeated become weather inside us.

There was a winter when my mind kept repeating one quiet storm: *this is too much; I can't do this.* Every time the sentence arrived, my body braced—shoulders climbed up, jaw tightened, breath went shallow. The room didn't change; I did. The sentence set the forecast.

One night, I tried something smaller, kinder. Not a thunderclap mantra—just a shift in tone I can actually breathe:

I am here. I am safe. I am meeting this night with enough.

The first repetition is wooden. By the fifth, my chest loosens. By the tenth, the room feels wider. I am not erasing difficulty; I am finishing the sentence with steadiness. I am discovering that I don't just speak words—words are speaking to me.

Affirmations are not slogans. They are breath-shaped choices. With every inhale, I am receiving the state I am naming; with every exhale, I am releasing the one I am done carrying. This isn't pretending. It is practicing—training the nervous system to return to ground, again and again, until ground is easier to find.

So we are beginning here: learning to craft sentences we can truly breathe, not force. Learning to let those sentences travel with our inhalations and exhalations until they settle into muscle, posture, and day. If Chapter Four is anchoring presence, Chapter Five is giving that presence a voice—warm, honest, and strong.

When we are ready, we turn the page into why these sentences work—how brain, breath, and centuries of spiritual practice are all agreeing on the same quiet truth: what we repeat, we are becoming.

From Breath to Word – Completing the Circle

The pause of breath is giving us an anchor. Meditation gives us presence. Visualization gives us direction. But the circle is not complete until words are spoken into the breath.

Affirmations are the flame — burning the pattern into the nervous system, feeding the seeds you planted with visualization. Every time you breathe words into your body, you tell your nervous system: *this is who I am becoming.*

Why Affirmations Work (and Why Flimsy Ones Don't)

The brain is always sculpting. Every thought I repeat is pressing into soft clay; every repetition makes the groove deeper. Neuroscience calls this neuroplasticity—neurons that fire together wire together.

When I repeat, *I can't handle this*, my brain is obedient: it wires for dread, collects proof, heightens stress hormones. When I repeat, *I am steady enough for this step*, the same obedience works in my favor. The groove reshapes; stress responses can ease and attention shifts. Mind calms.

The brain's attention systems (often described via the reticular activating system) help decide what to highlight, what to dim. If I am muttering *winter is miserable*, the RAS dutifully scans for grey skies, icy sidewalks, sharp winds. If I am whispering, *I am noticing small warmth*, the RAS shifts its filter—I am catching the blanket at my feet, the neighbor's nod, the patch of sun at 2:14 p.m. The outer world hasn't changed. The inner filter has.

Psychology agrees. Self-affirmation theory, pioneered by Claude Steele, shows that when people affirm values they actually hold—family, kindness, learning—they don't crumble under stress. They regulate better, recover faster. Their sense of self remains intact even under pressure. Brain imaging studies suggest that value-anchored self-affirmation engages regions involved in self-related processing and emotion regulation. The body is registering affirmation, not as fluff, but as signal.

And spirit has known this for centuries.

- In yoga, mantra is vibration as much as meaning. Om repeated is not wordplay—it is rhythm training breath, heart, and mind to hum together.
- In Christianity, prayers repeated daily—*The Lord's Prayer*, *The Jesus Prayer*—sink beneath words to become heartbeat.
- In Islam, *dhikr* (remembrance) repeats God's names until the inner noise thins and presence steadies.
- In Indigenous traditions, chants around winter fires remind people of courage and continuity. Gratitude and identity are sung into the night.

The thread is the same: repetition is medicine. Words are not ornaments; they are instruments.

But here is the key: hollow affirmations collapse. Whispering *I love every blizzard* through clenched teeth is not affirmation—it is performance. What works is believable stretch: a sentence I can breathe today, even if it only shifts me one degree closer to warmth.

Affirmations are not about pretending. They are about practicing—about choosing sentences that the breath can carry until the nervous system begins believing.

Reflection Prompt: Write down three of your values right now–not in theory, but what feels alive this season. For each, craft one affirmation in present continuous form.

- Value: Kindness → *I am treating myself kindly as I walk through winter.*
- Value: Growth → *I am learning something small each day, even in the dark season.*
- Value: Connection → *I am bringing warmth to those I meet, even in long nights.*

Rules for Living Sentences

Think of an affirmation as a winter mug. It must be something you can hold—warm enough to comfort, solid enough to support, not so hot it burns your hands. A good sentence is the same: believable, breathable, steady.

1. Present Continuous

Your nervous system relaxes into *now*. Future-tense sentences (*I will be calm*) postpone peace. Static present tense (*I am calm*) sometimes rings hollow. Present continuous is alive: *I am breathing calm. I am softening into rest. I am noticing warmth.* The action is happening in this moment.

2. Positive Direction

The brain is clumsy with negation. Say *I am not anxious* and "anxious" is the word that sticks. Say *I am breathing steadiness,* and the nervous system leans into that. Aim the sentence where you want to go, not what you want to avoid.

3. Sensory Anchoring

Flat words slide off. Embodied words sink in. *I am opening the blinds inside my chest. I am warming my hands with breath.* These images give your body something to recognize. The nervous system believes faster when the sentence is paired with sensation.

4. Believable Stretch

If February has you muttering, *I despise this season,* don't leap to *I am loving winter.* That is a sentence too tall. It topples. Instead: *I am opening to one good winter moment today.* That one step creates a foothold. Repetition builds the ladder.

5. Consistency over Novelty

The mind is tempted by variety: a new sentence each morning. But the body changes through repetition. One true sentence, breathed for twenty-one days, rewires more than twenty-one half-hearted ones. Depth beats novelty. Pick one, maybe two, and live with them until they shape you.

6. Compassion in Adjustment

If your chosen sentence catches in your throat, don't bully yourself. Adjust. *I am resting easily* might need to soften into *I am allowing myself brief rests.* When you find a version that makes your breath drop deeper into your belly, you've found your fit.

"An affirmation is not a slogan.
It is a sentence the body can believe,
repeated until the heart remembers."

Reflection Prompt: Sit by a window. Place a hand on your chest and one on your belly. Breathe slowly until your shoulders drop. Ask gently: *What do I need to be saying to myself this winter?* Listen for a word–patience, warmth, courage. Shape it into a sentence in present continuous. Whisper it once. Notice: did your body resist, or did it soften? Rewrite until it fits.

Affirmation Breath – Words Entering the Body

Affirmations need breath to take root. Without breath, they remain surface-level. With breath, they enter the bloodstream. They travel from mouth to muscle, from idea to atmosphere.

Think of breath as the carrier wave. The sentence is the message, but breath is the frequency that carries it into the nervous system.

How to Practice

1. Sit steady. Choose a seat where your spine can lengthen without strain. Place one hand on your chest, the other on your belly.
2. Inhale (four counts). Breathe in through the nose, saying silently: *I am receiving light / I am receiving calm / I am receiving warmth.*
3. Hold (two counts). Not tense—just enough to let the words land. Feel them settle in the chest.
4. Exhale (six counts). Through the mouth, whisper softly: *I am releasing hurry / I am releasing heaviness / I am releasing tension.*
5. Repeat 7–10 rounds. Let the counting slow you. Let the rhythm carry the sentence deeper each cycle.

If the mind wanders, do not scold it. Return to the next inhale. This is not about forcing the mind still; it is about letting breath braid with words until they feel inseparable.

Why It Works

- Biology: Inhaling activates the sympathetic nervous system (alerting), exhaling activates the parasympathetic (calming). By elongating the exhale, you cue safety. Adding words directs the nervous system toward a chosen state.
- Psychology: Pairing a sentence with breath engages both cognition and body, strengthening memory and belief.
- Spirit: Across traditions, breath is sacred—ruach, prana, pneuma. Pairing breath with words makes the affirmation prayerful, lived.

Client Story – Mark's Morning Shift

Mark, a professional in his late thirties, described mornings as "a fight I lost before I even stood up." His mind raced: *Too much to do. I'll never catch up.*

We chose a simple pair:

- Inhale: *I am receiving light.*
- Exhale: *I am releasing heaviness.*

Day one, he said it felt forced. Day seven, neutral. Day fourteen, he emailed: *I don't wake in a fight anymore. I wake in a room I recognize.* By day twenty-one, the sentence had evolved: *I am breathing like someone I trust.*

Mark's story is not about magic—it's about rehearsal. Breath carried words into muscle memory until mornings became less about battle, more about belonging.

Reflection Prompt: Write your own inhale/exhale pair. Keep it in present continuous and make it believable.

Examples:

- Inhale: *I am receiving calm.* Exhale: *I am releasing tension.*
- Inhale: *I am receiving focus.* Exhale: *I am releasing noise.*
- Inhale: *I am receiving joy.* Exhale: *I am releasing gloom.*

Practice daily for 21 days. Each evening, note: How did the sentence land today?

"Breath is how words stop being ideas and start becoming atmosphere."

Daily Rituals That Make Words Real

Affirmations don't live on paper. They live in repetition, in breath, in the pauses where life unfolds. They need touch, rhythm, light, and small daily anchors. These rituals weave your chosen sentence into your nervous system until it's no longer just an idea — it becomes weather you can walk inside.

Morning Mirror

Each morning, the mirror already waits for you. Fog it with your breath — make the invisible visible. Then, with your fingertip, write your sentence:

- *I am being steady.*
- *I am being kind to myself.*

Say it three times while watching your reflection receive it. At first, it may feel awkward, even artificial. But repetition is a form of faith. Over weeks, your reflection begins to change atmosphere. You are no longer just brushing your teeth — you are rehearsing self-trust.

You can also do this without fogging the mirror: simply meet your gaze and speak your affirmation gently, as if you're reminding an old friend of something true.

Pocket Card

Take a small card. Write your sentence in your own handwriting. Slip it into your coat pocket. Each time you reach for your keys, touch it. Do not rush—let your fingers rest on it. Touch is primal; your body remembers what your mind forgets. This small pause interrupts autopilot and re-roots you in your chosen weather.

Walking Mantra

On a snowy sidewalk or in a quiet hallway, pace your sentence into your steps.

- Left step: first half.
- Right step: second half.

I am carrying light → into this room.
I am allowing rest → without apology.

The rhythm of steps becomes rhythm of belief. After ten minutes, notice how posture itself changes the sentence—and how the sentence changes posture.

Candle Close

At night, light a candle. Whisper your sentence three times: once for yourself, once for someone you love, once for a stranger who might need it tonight. Blow it out like a lantern into the dark. Sleep inside the echo.

This ritual is small, but it carries ancient resonance—fire has always been the witness to our prayers.

Three Winters, Three Voices

These stories show how ordinary people wove affirmations into daily rituals until the sentences reshaped their winters—and themselves.

Hannah (nurse)
Twelve-hour shifts drained her body; guilt punished her for needing rest. Her sentence: *I am being allowed rest.*
Week one: she spoke it like apology.
Week two: she spoke it like experiment.
Week three: she said it and felt her spine soften. Rest was no longer guilt—it was medicine.

Ben (founder)
Ben was a startup founder who lived by momentum. In summer, he thrived on long days and late nights, sprinting from one idea to the next. But when winter came, the darkness felt like a wall. He judged himself by output, and every sluggish morning felt like failure.

His sentence became: *I am being enough for today.*

At first, it tasted bitter, like defeat. He repeated it anyway — in the mirror, on walks to his office, in the silent moments before logging onto Zoom. Slowly, the words began to work. Instead of forcing twelve-hour marathons, he built measured days: one true step, one solid meeting, one intentional pause. His panic quieted. His work didn't collapse — in fact, his decisions sharpened. "Enough," he told me one afternoon, "turned out to be more than enough."

Olivia (student)
Olivia had moved north for graduate school, leaving behind the endless sun of her coastal hometown. By November, she felt betrayed by the sky. "I hate winter," she muttered a dozen times a day — to classmates, to baristas, to herself. Each repetition made the days heavier.

We shifted it to: *I am finding one thing to like today.*

At first it felt forced. One day she laughed at a ridiculous hat on a passing dog. Another day it was the taste of hot soup between classes. By late January, she was catching shafts of sunlight on her desk at exactly 2:14

p.m. By February, she no longer had to search so hard. "I meet winter with curiosity," she said one evening, surprising herself with sincerity. Winter didn't get warmer, but her language did. And the language changed her life.

Reflection Prompt: Write your chosen sentence on three surfaces:

- Fogged bathroom mirror.
- Phone lock screen.
- A card in your coat pocket.

Rehearse it in the morning, walk it at midday, whisper it at night. Track one moment each day when the sentence changed your mood, posture, or response.

"Affirmations need breath, but they also need handles. Rituals are how your hands hold your words until your heart believes them."

Beyond Winter – Affirmations in Every Area of Life

Winter is training ground. Once you practice affirmations here, you can carry them into every season. Think of the sentences as seeds that travel with you.

Career

- I am bringing clarity into my work.
- I am creating with courage, even in small steps.
- I am being open to learning from each challenge.

Love & Relationships

- I am giving love freely.
- I am receiving love openly.
- I am being present with those I cherish.

Health & Body

- I am nourishing my body with kindness.
- I am resting as medicine.
- I am being gentle with my limits and grateful for my strength.

Growth & Spirit

- I am trusting my path.
- I am meeting life with curiosity.
- I am expanding with each season, not just surviving them.

Reflection Prompt: Take one deep breath. Write three authentic affirmations–one for career, one for relationships, one for self. Make sure each begins in the present continuous. Say them aloud once. Notice: Which one makes your shoulders drop? Which one makes your chest feel warm? That is the sentence your body already believes.

"Affirmations are not posters on the wall. They are living sentences you breathe into your days until they become your climate."

The 21-Day Winter Practice

Affirmations only grow roots when you live with them. Repetition carves grooves in the brain, and three weeks is long enough to etch a new rhythm. Think of this practice as a personal winter experiment: twenty-one days of choosing one sentence, breathing it, carrying it, and closing your day with it.

Daily Flow

1. Breathe your sentence (2–5 minutes, morning using the 4-2-6 breath)

- Sit comfortably, hand on chest and belly.
- Use **Affirmation Breath**: Inhale for 4 counts → say silently: *I am receiving calm/light/steadiness.*
- Hold for 2 counts → let the words settle.
- Exhale for 6 counts → whisper: *I am releasing hurry/heaviness/tension.*
- Repeat 7–10 rounds.
- This is not performance. It is atmosphere-making.

2. Carry your sentence (throughout the day)

- Keep your sentence on a pocket card or your phone lock screen.
- Touch it before emails, before difficult conversations, before stepping outside.
- Let the words interrupt autopilot and bring you back.

3. Close with your sentence (evening)

- Write it once in your journal, slowly.
- Or whisper it before bed, letting it be the last vibration your body hears.
- Optional: Light a candle and speak the sentence once for yourself, once for someone you love, once for a stranger. Blow it out like sending a lantern into the dark.

Weekly Reflection

Every seventh day, pause and write:

- *What small shift did I notice this week?*
  Maybe it was softer shoulders, slower mornings, a kinder reply to yourself. Small is the point. Small is how winter turns.

Troubleshooting: When the Sentence Resists

- **If it feels too big:** Shrink it.
  - "I love winter" → "I am being open to one good winter moment today."
- **If it feels flat:** Add imagery.
  - "I am calm" → "I am warming my chest with breath."
- **If it feels heavy:** Pause. Breathe silently. Return later with a gentler phrase.
  - "I am full of joy" may need to soften into "I am noticing small joys."

Nothing is wrong. You are simply learning your body's mouth-shape for truth.

Reflection Page: My 21-Day Winter Practice

- Write your chosen sentence at the top of the page.
- Beneath it, create 21 small circles. Each day you pair the sentence with breath, fill one circle.
- If you miss a day, don't erase. Place a dot in the margin and continue. Consistency is stronger than perfection.

"Small sentences, repeated daily, become climates strong enough to carry you through storms."

Compassionate Troubleshooting: When Sentences Resist

Not every affirmation will land right away. Some will feel wooden, others too sharp, others out of reach. That doesn't mean you're failing; it means you're refining.

- If the words feel too big → shrink them.
  - *I adore winter → I am being open to one good winter moment today.*
- If the words feel flat → add image or sensation.
  - *I am calm → I am warming my chest with breath.*
- If the words feel heavy → pause. Breathe silently. Anchor in a Root Visualization or simply place a hand on your chest. Return later with a gentler phrase.

Affirmations are not a performance. They are practice. Think of them less like slogans and more like seeds: some sprout quickly, others take time under snow.

Closing Practice – Words as Rooms

Affirmations are not just sentences. They are rooms you live inside. Some are cramped with fear; others open windows you didn't know were there. This practice lets you build your own room of breath and word.

How to Practice

1. Sit near a window.
2. Place one hand on your chest, one on your belly.
3. Inhale for four counts: *I am steady.*
4. Hold softly for two counts.
5. Exhale for six counts: *I am letting go my haste / hurry.*
6. Repeat until breath and words fuse.
7. When ready, let the words fall away. Notice the residue: a warmth in your palms, a loosening in your shoulders, the sense that the room itself feels different.

Whisper once more, like sealing a letter: *I meet this season with enough.*

Simply close your eyes. Watch how the smoke or the darkness curls around you. The sentence remains, glowing inwardly.

Transition Into Gratitude

If affirmations are the inhale—drawing light and steadiness into your body—then gratitude is the exhale. Gratitude takes the words you've cultivated inside and extends them outward, to life, to others, to the world.

This is where we turn next. Gratitude is not another checklist—it is a way of warming your inner room and inviting others to share its light.

"Affirmations change the weather within.
Gratitude lets that weather spill into the world."

CHAPTER FIVE SUMMARY - WORDS WE ARE BREATHING: THE POWER OF AFFIRMATIONS

Key Insight

Breath anchors the body; words give that anchor a voice. The sentences we repeat become the weather within us. When aligned with real values, affirmations stop being slogans and become breath-shaped choices that gently retrain the nervous system toward steadiness, warmth, and self-trust.

Core Metaphors

- Weather Inside: Each phrase sets an inner forecast – "I can't do this" is a storm; "I am steady enough for this step" is a clearing sky.
- Winter Mug: A good affirmation is like a mug you can hold – warm enough to comfort, solid enough to support, not so hot it burns your hands.
- Chants Across Traditions: Mantra, prayer, dhikr, winter fires – all use repetition as medicine, words as instruments rather than ornaments.

Rituals of Living Sentences

- Affirmation Breath – Pair a believable inhale/exhale sentence with slow breathing to carry it into muscle memory.
- Morning Mirror – Fog the mirror with your breath; write or whisper your sentence as you meet your reflection.
- Pocket Card – Keep your sentence on a small card; touch it before tasks to interrupt autopilot.
- Walking Mantra – Pace the sentence into your steps: left foot first half, right foot second half.

- Candle Close – Speak the sentence once for yourself, once for someone you love, once for a stranger; blow it out like a lantern into the dark.

Reflection Prompts

- List three values alive in you this season; craft one present-continuous affirmation for each.
- Sit by a window, hand on chest and belly. Ask: "What do I need to be saying to myself this winter?" Shape it into a sentence you can actually breathe.
- Write your chosen affirmation on three surfaces – mirror, lock screen, pocket card – and track one moment each day when it changed your posture, mood, or response.

Closing Meditation Mantra

"Small sentences, breathed daily, become climates strong enough to carry you through storms."

CHAPTER SIX

Winter Gratitude: Warming the Heart in Cold Days

Thankfulness isn't a mood; it's a muscle that makes any moment wider."

"There is always something to be thankful for."

At first glance, the words look like something printed on a mug or stitched onto a pillow. Easy to skim, easier to dismiss. But when winter presses in—when the nights stretch too long, when the mornings feel heavy, when silence feels less like peace and more like weight—these words stop being decoration. They become lifelines.

Gratitude is not pretending difficulty away. It is not painting over hardship with cheer. It is choosing to speak differently—to yourself, and to the world—even when the cold is sharp, even when the light feels scarce.

Earlier, we spoke of affirmations, those inner sentences that change the weather of the body. Gratitude is the continuation of that work, only now the conversation moves outward. Affirmations anchor you inside; gratitude opens you to dialogue with life itself. If affirmations are the inhale, gratitude is the exhale.

I remember a client showed me `a meme of a person on Instagram, shoulders hunched against the cold, laughing as he shoveled snow: *"At least we don't have alligators. Or hurricanes. Or snakes falling from trees."* He meant it as a joke, but the shift was profound. In that moment, he wasn't wrestling with winter; he was reframing it. His sentence turned complaint into context, heaviness into perspective.

Gratitude doesn't say, "This is easy." It whispers, "Even here, there is something still being given."

And this is where our practice deepens: learning to find gratitude not only for warm blankets and mugs of tea, but also for the resilience we discover in ourselves, for the breath that never leaves, for the small sparks that light us in the dark—and learning to carry that practice far beyond winter, into every season of life.

Why Gratitude Belongs to Winter

Gratitude is effortless in summer. The world offers it to you on a silver platter. The sky sings at dawn, warmth lingers late, fruit spills from baskets at the market. You don't even notice the thank-you forming in your chest—it slips out naturally, as easy as breath.

But in winter, gratitude is not automatic. The birds are quiet. The markets are sparse. The days narrow and the cold presses against your skin. Here, gratitude becomes discipline. And precisely because it takes effort, it grows stronger.

Winter gratitude is a kind of training. It teaches your eyes to seek sparks in the dark: the golden spill of light through a window, the softness of a scarf, the miracle of your own exhale visible in the air. It teaches your body to recognize what is still here: warmth, shelter, breath, human presence. It is not about having everything—it is about noticing something.

And science, once again, affirms what the soul has always known. Neuroimaging studies suggest that gratitude activates regions of the prefrontal cortex associated with perspective and emotion regulation. It's also linked to increased dopamine and serotonin activity — neurotransmitters that influence mood balance. Psychological studies indicate that regular gratitude journaling can help lower perceived stress, improve sleep quality, and strengthen emotional resilience.

But my favorite part is this: gratitude changes what the brain sees. Your brain's attention systems — often described through the Reticular Activating System (RAS) — take subtle cues from focus and language. Tell it *"everything is awful,"* and it collects proof like a diligent servant. Tell it *"I am grateful for warmth,"* and it begins to highlight warmth everywhere: blankets, steam rising from a mug, a neighbor waving as he salts the sidewalk. Gratitude doesn't erase the cold. It simply trains your brain to notice what still carries heat.

And here's the secret that expands beyond winter: if you can practice gratitude when the world feels stingy with its gifts, you will carry that practice into every season. Gratitude in summer is easy. Gratitude in winter is mastery.

Gratitude as Dialogue with Winter

Think of every complaint as an unfinished sentence. A half-uttered thought, waiting for you to finish it. Gratitude is how you complete it—not by denying the first half, but by adding the second.

- *"It's so cold."*
  → *"Yes, and that cold makes me savor warmth in ways summer never teaches."*
- *"It gets dark too early."*
  → *"Yes, and this darkness invites me to rest, to remember the stars."*
- *"The snow is so heavy to shovel."*
  → *"Yes, and I am grateful my body is still strong enough to lift it, one breath, one scoop at a time."*

This is not about painting over reality. It is about rewriting the ending of your dialogue with life. Complaints left unfinished turn into loops, repeating and tightening. Gratitude completes the sentence, lets it rest, and gives your nervous system closure.

One client once came to me with the mantra, *"I can't handle this anymore."* It was her winter sentence, spoken every evening as she returned to a dark apartment after long hours at work. We didn't try to silence it. We finished it. She began with: *"I can't handle this anymore… and yet I am grateful I kept going today."* Later: *"…and I am grateful for the tea waiting in my cupboard."* Later still: *"…and I am grateful for my resilience that keeps showing up."*

After a few weeks, she told me, "I still say the first part, but now it doesn't feel like a wall. It feels like a doorway."

That is what gratitude does. It doesn't erase the cold or the dark. It adds a new clause, a softer ending, a reminder that even here, life is still giving.

And beyond winter? This practice becomes a universal skill.

- *"This project failed."* → *"Yes, and I am grateful for what it taught me."*
- *"This relationship ended."* → *"Yes, and I am grateful I learned what love feels like."*
- *"This season is heavy."* → *"Yes, and I am grateful it is shaping me into someone stronger, kinder, more awake."*

Gratitude doesn't erase hardship. It reframes it. It gives you back authorship of your own sentences.

Gratitude Across Cultures – Wisdom in Harsh Climates

Gratitude is not new. It has always been survival. Across cultures, especially in the harshest climates, people learned that gratitude was not something ornamental you wrote in a journal at the end of a nice day. It was how you kept going when the day itself was not nice at all.

Sámi Fires (Northern Scandinavia)

On endless Arctic nights, Sámi families gathered around fires that were more than warmth — they were sanctuaries. Around those flames, blessings were named: for reindeer that gave meat and hides, for birch trees that bent but did not break in storms, for neighbors who showed up. Storytelling itself was gratitude, because each tale reminded the listeners: *we are not alone in the dark.* Gratitude here was not about comfort. It was about connection — the warmth of belonging.

Inuit Humor

Ethnographic records describe how some Inuit communities used play and humor — including breath and song games — to build warmth and connection through long winters. Living in some of the most unforgiving landscapes, they practiced gratitude through laughter. Children played "breath games," families created playful skits, teasing songs echoed in tents and igloos. To laugh together was to say: *I am glad you are here with me tonight.* Gratitude wasn't spoken as thank you, but embodied in shared joy, even in the coldest dark. Humor became a survival ritual — proof that the human spirit can thaw even when the world is frozen.

Norwegian Friluftsliv

In Norway, there is a saying: *there is no bad weather, only bad clothing.* Gratitude takes the form of *friluftsliv* — "open-air living." Even in January, people bundle up and go out to ski, to sip coffee on park benches, to walk forest paths under moonlight. The cold itself becomes something to thank, because it sharpens the senses and keeps aliveness awake. Gratitude here is not for what shelters you from winter, but for what winter itself offers.

Danish Hygge

In Denmark, gratitude is found indoors through *hygge* — the art of coziness. Candles flicker in windows, blankets pile on laps, hot drinks and laughter spill across living rooms. Gratitude here is about cherishing the ordinary: noticing the small flame, the soft wool, the familiar face across the table. Hygge teaches us that gratitude does not always roar; sometimes it whispers in tiny comforts.

Icelandic Mindset

Psychologist Kari Leibowitz calls it the "positive wintertime mindset." Icelanders, facing some of the longest nights on Earth, reframe winter as magical rather than miserable. Festivals erupt in the darkest weeks. Music, poetry, fish stew shared with neighbors — winter becomes not a curse but a canvas. Gratitude here is cultural software. It is how people continue to thrive, not despite winter, but with winter.

Indian Traditions: Gratitude to the Elements

Beyond the Arctic, Indian philosophy expands gratitude beyond season to the very foundations of existence. Gratitude is not occasional; it is elemental.

- **Surya (Sun):** Daily prayers and *Surya Namaskar* (sun salutations) honor the light that sustains all life. Even when the sky is grey, bowing reminds you: *I still receive, even when I cannot see.*
- **Prithvi (Earth):** Harvest festivals like Pongal and Makar Sankranti honor soil, cattle, and tools. Gratitude becomes ritualized interdependence: *I do not thrive alone.*

- **Jala (Water):** Rivers like Ganga are revered as mothers. Offerings remind us to give back to what sustains us. Gratitude here is a daily covenant with life itself.
- **Vayu (Air):** In *pranayama* practice, each breath is received as gift and returned in thanks. Every inhale is receiving; every exhale is releasing. Breath itself becomes prayer.
- **Agni (Fire):** In yajna rituals, flames are fed with food, ghee, and flowers — a reminder that fire is not only warmth, but presence. Gratitude is enacted by returning a portion of what we take.
- **Akasha (Space):** Space holds all. The sky, silence, the room inside the ribcage. Gratitude here is reverence for capacity — for the quiet that allows experience to unfold.

These traditions, whether around Arctic fires or Indian temples, carry one truth: gratitude is not ornamental. It is resilience. It turns scarcity into enough, and enough into blessing.

And you don't need to live in Norway, Sweden or India to practice this. Lighting a candle tonight can echo Sámi firelight. Sharing a joke at dinner can mirror Inuit humor. Stepping outside for five minutes of air can be your own *friluftsliv*. As you wrap your hands around the first cup of coffee, let it be your moment to greet the light, within and without. Gratitude isn't found in grand gestures; it lives quietly in small awakenings. Gratitude is universal. It just waits for you to notice.

Practices for Winter Gratitude

I repeat these are not chores to tick off. They are invitations to step differently into your day. Think of them as doorways: each one opens you to a dialogue of gratitude, not just with winter, but with life itself.

1. The Winter Gratitude Journal — Engraving Sparks in the Dark

Most of us know the classic advice: write three things you're grateful for. But in winter, we need something sharper, something more specific.

Instead of a generic list, ask: *What did winter give me today that summer never could?*

Maybe it was the silence of snow at dawn, where even the city held its breath. Maybe it was steam rising from your own breath on the glass, reminding you you're alive. Maybe it was the neighbor who shoveled your walk without asking. Write it slowly, as if engraving it. Over time, the pages become a quilt, stitched with moments of warmth you might have missed.

2. The Mug Ritual — Beginning with Warmth
Every winter morning begins the same way: cold air, heavy clothes, sluggishness. But then you wrap your hands around a mug — tea, coffee, cocoa. That mug is more than caffeine; it is warmth embodied.

Before you sip, pause. Feel the heat in your palms. Watch the steam curl. Whisper one sentence of gratitude: *I am grateful for warmth in my hands. I am grateful for breath in my chest.*

This ritual takes 10 seconds. But it changes the architecture of the day. You begin not with rushing, but with a sip of gratitude.

3. The Gratitude Walk — Turning Steps into Sentences
Winter tempts us to stay indoors, but step outside and listen. Each crunch of snow under your boots, each breath of cold air filling your lungs, is a chance to notice. As you walk, pair each step with a sentence: *I am grateful for this inhale. I am grateful for this exhale.*

Look at the bare branches, the fog of your own breath, the way light refracts differently in cold air. You are not just walking — you are collecting small treasures. After ten minutes, the body feels different. You didn't just move through winter; you walked through gratitude.

4. The Mirror Gratitude — Honoring Yourself
Winter can make us harshest with ourselves — critical of our exhaustion, impatient with our moods. That's why one of the most radical practices is

this: stand in front of a mirror. Look into your own eyes. And say: *I am grateful for the one who endured to stand here.*

Watch your face as the words land. At first it may feel awkward, even defiant. But keep at it. Over weeks, your reflection will begin to carry a different atmosphere. Gratitude softens the way you see the world — and the way you see yourself.

5. The Gratitude Note— Multiplying Warmth
Gratitude multiplies when spoken. Once a week, choose someone who made winter softer for you and write them a note. It doesn't need to be profound: *Thank you for making the best hot chocolate. Thank you for always texting me a joke when the sky is grey.*

You may not know it, but your note could be the fire in someone else's long night. Gratitude is never just yours. It always spills over.

6. Humor as Gratitude's Cousin — Smiling Through the Cold
Some days, gratitude feels too heavy a word. That's when humor comes in as gratitude's lighter cousin. Humor is how gratitude puts on boots.

Snow piling up on your driveway? At least no alligators are lurking there. Frozen pipes? At least no hurricanes are ripping through the roof. It may sound small, but this reframing keeps despair from taking the last word. Laughter itself is a thank you — a recognition that joy still exists.

Client Story – From Winter Practice to Life Practice

One client came to me in late December, brittle with deadlines and dread. "What's there to be thankful for?" she asked. "It's freezing, I'm exhausted, and I hate the dark."

We began small. Night one, her journal read: "I guess I'm grateful for coffee." By the end of week one: "I'm grateful for my daughter's hug before school." By week two: "I'm grateful for silence after dinner."

Her complaints dulled, but the deeper shift came in spring. A promotion slipped to a colleague. Old her would have spiraled into resentment. New her paused, opened her journal, and wrote: *I am grateful this sting is pointing me to a clearer path.*

Instead of shrinking, she asked for feedback, applied it, and within six months shaped a role more aligned with her strengths. By summer, her gratitude pages included lines like: "I'm grateful I didn't get what I thought I wanted first. It revealed what I actually wanted."

Gratitude didn't just carry her through winter. It reshaped how she faced setbacks, success, and herself.

Beyond Winter – Gratitude as a Life Practice

Gratitude is not meant to retire when spring arrives. If anything, winter teaches us the discipline that carries into brighter months. When the days lengthen, gratitude becomes easier again — but without practice, it also becomes invisible. You stop noticing the ordinary blessings that once anchored you.

Think of winter gratitude as training with weights on. If you can find thanks in February's silence, then gratitude in June's sunlight will feel effortless. The practice builds muscles you carry everywhere.

Gratitude for the Self

It begins with you. Noticing the resilience in your own reflection, the breath that still moves, the body that still shows up. Say: *I am thanking myself for keeping on. I am honoring the small acts that carried me here.*

This self-directed gratitude is not vanity — it is fuel. Without it, every act of giving turns into depletion. With it, giving becomes overflow.

Gratitude for Work and Career

Deadlines, disappointments, promotions gained or lost — gratitude reframes them. One client began writing: *I am grateful for this failure pointing me to a clearer strength.* Another said: *I am grateful for the chance to grow in ways I didn't plan.*

Practical prompts:

- *I am grateful for the skills I am practicing each day.*
- *I am grateful for the colleagues who challenge and shape me.*
- *I am grateful that my work gives me a chance to create, contribute, or learn.*

Gratitude does not ignore ambition; it anchors it in perspective.

Gratitude in Relationships

In love, friendship, or family, gratitude is a bridge. It turns assumptions into appreciation. Instead of *they should know I care,* gratitude says it out loud: *thank you for standing with me in this.*

Practical prompts:

- *I am grateful for the laughter I share with...*
- *I am grateful for patience given when I faltered.*
- *I am grateful for ordinary moments – meals, messages, gestures – that would be easy to miss.*

When spoken aloud, gratitude softens tension and multiplies connection.

Gratitude for Health and Body

Even when imperfect, your body is carrying you. Winter aches may tempt complaint, but gratitude reframes: *thank you, legs, for walking me through another day; thank you, breath, for arriving without me asking.*

Practical prompts:

- *I am grateful for the strength to move through today.*
- *I am grateful for the rest my body receives.*
- *I am grateful for the ways healing is happening, even unseen.*

Gratitude for Growth and Spirit

Every challenge, delay, or detour is also a teacher. Gratitude here is not naïve optimism. Instead, it's reverence for the mystery of becoming.

Prompts:

- *I am grateful for what this setback revealed about me.*
- *I am grateful for the questions I'm still carrying.*
- *I am grateful for the unseen seeds already growing beneath the soil of today.*

Reflection Prompt: A Breath of Thanks in All Areas

Take one deep breath. On the inhale, whisper: *I am receiving.* On the exhale: *I am grateful.* Then write one authentic affirmation of gratitude in each area:

- Career → *I am grateful for the clarity I am building in my work.*
- Love → *I am grateful for the ways love arrives, even in small gestures.*
- Health → *I am grateful for my body's quiet strength.*
- Growth → *I am grateful for the path unfolding, even when I can't see far ahead.*

Let them be simple, present continuous, and true.

Closing Reflection – Gratitude as Bridge to Joy

If affirmations are the inhale and gratitude is the exhale, then joy is the smile that appears between breaths. Gratitude grounds you in the present while quietly training your eyes to notice beauty. And beauty, when noticed, becomes joy.

Tonight, before you sleep, whisper one thing you are grateful for. It does not need to be profound. It only needs to be honest.

"Tonight, I am being grateful for ____. And that is enough."

This soft landing prepares us for what comes next: joy not as fleeting happiness, but as a practice — the natural outgrowth of gratitude lived fully.

Reflection: Winter Gratitude

Daily Log

Today I am grateful for:

1.

2.

3.

Reframing Practice

Complaint: __________

Gratitude reframe: __________

Weekly Reflection

- What themes keep repeating? People? Comfort? Nature? Self?
- How has my winter dialogue shifted since I began?

Beyond Winter

- What gratitude do I carry into spring and summer?

CHAPTER SIX SUMMARY - WINTER GRATITUDE: WARMING THE HEART IN COLD DAYS

Key Insight

Gratitude in winter is not decoration; it's endurance. In bright seasons, thankfulness flows without effort. But in the cold, gratitude becomes a discipline – a deliberate search for sparks in the dark. Practiced this way, it gently retrains the nervous system, steadies mood, and teaches the mind to notice warmth even when light feels scarce.

Core Metaphors

- Finishing the Sentence: Complaints are half-finished thoughts; gratitude adds the second clause that turns walls into doorways.
- Sámi Fires & Inuit Humor: In harsh climates, gratitude is not ornamental – it's connection, survival, and shared joy.
- Winter Training: Thankfulness in scarcity builds the muscles you carry into every season.

Practices of Winter Gratitude

- Winter Gratitude Journal – Ask, "What did winter give me today that summer never could?" Write one or two specifics each night.
- The Mug Ritual – Before your first sip, pause to feel the heat in your hands and whisper one sentence of thanks.
- Gratitude Walk – Pair each step or breath outside with: "I am grateful for this inhale… this exhale."
- Mirror Gratitude – Look at yourself and say: "I'm grateful for the one who endured to stand here."
- Gratitude Letter – Once a week, thank someone who softened your winter.

- Humor as Gratitude's Cousin – Let laughter be a thank-you when words feel too heavy.

Reflection Prompts

- Write three things winter gave you today that another season wouldn't.
- Take one common complaint and finish it with a gratitude clause.
- Who or what softened your day this week? Write a short thank-you note – even if you don't send it.

Closing Mantra

"I am noticing small sparks of warmth. I am grateful, even here."

CHAPTER SEVEN

From Inner Critic to Inner Coach

(Self-Compassion as the Missing Practice)
Let your inner voice be the tone you'd use with a child you cherish.

Prelude: When Winter Threw Me Off Track

One winter I thought I finally cracked the code. I had my rituals in place: breathing each morning before the inbox flooded, stepping outside to catch slivers of light, writing affirmations that steadied me. My days felt grounded, my nights softer. I told myself: *This time, I won't get derailed.*

But then came a single week that unraveled everything.

It started innocently — one late night of work, a deadline that pushed me past midnight. The next morning I skipped my breath practice, telling myself I'd "make it up later." That afternoon, a back-to-back wall of meetings left no room for my walk. By midweek, the sky was endless grey and drizzle. I glanced at my shoes by the door and muttered: *what's the point?*

By Friday night, I was right back in an old rhythm: scrolling too late, skipping rituals, scolding myself for slipping. And that's when the voice returned.

It didn't shout at first. It whispered. "You always fail." "You talk about calm, but can't even live it." "You're weak."

Each phrase landed like ice against the ribs. My shoulders tensed, my jaw tightened, my breath went shallow. The critic wasn't new — it was an old companion, waiting for just such a crack in my resolve. And once it found the opening, it poured in.

We all know this voice. In winter, it often grows louder. Darkness presses in, patience thins, energy dips — and the critic steps in like a harsh taskmaster, insisting that one missed ritual means all progress is lost.

But that week something shifted. I didn't try to argue with it or drown it out. Instead, I asked a smaller question: *What's one thing I can be grateful for, even in this mess?*

I picked up my journal and wrote a single line: *I'm grateful I noticed.*

Not a long list. Not a performance. Just that. But as my pen scratched the page, I felt my shoulders drop half an inch. The weather inside me shifted. Gratitude didn't erase my slip-ups, but it softened them. It turned the critic's accusation into the coach's encouragement. It reminded me that noticing itself was progress.

That was the week I realized: the journey through winter isn't about silencing the critic. It's about retraining it. The critic is part of me — but it can be reshaped into a coach. And the tool that makes this possible isn't willpower. It's self-compassion.

The Critic's Origins: Badly Programmed Protection

The critic's voice often sounds cruel, but beneath the sharpness it is trying — in its clumsy way — to protect you.

Think of our ancestors on a dark plain thousands of years ago. The one who lingered too long admiring the sunset might have been caught by the predator hiding in the shadows. Survival meant noticing threats before beauty. That vigilance became wired into us as what psychologists call *negativity bias.* Praise slips past like water, but criticism sticks like thorns. Our nervous system leans toward fear because, once upon a time, fear kept us alive.

That wiring still hums in us today. The critic is like an outdated alarm system — shrill, oversensitive, and convinced that scaring us is the only way to keep us safe. It doesn't know the difference between missing a morning ritual and being chased by a tiger. So it blares: *You failed. You're weak. Don't even try again.*

Research in neuroscience suggests how deep this groove runs.

- **Amygdala bias:** The amygdala, our brain's threat detector, reacts to criticism with a stronger, faster surge of cortisol than it does to praise.
- **Neuroplasticity:** Each time we repeat self-critical thoughts, we strengthen those neural pathways. The groove deepens, and the critic's voice arrives faster and is harder to ignore.

Psychologist Kristin Neff, whose work on self-compassion has reshaped modern psychology, explains it simply: the critic believes self-attacking will whip us into shape. But study after study shows the opposite. Self-compassion — not self-attack — fosters resilience, healthier motivation, and steadier effort. When people treat themselves with kindness, oxytocin rises, stress drops and their nervous system steadies.

Spiritual traditions have been saying the same thing for centuries.

- In the **Ancient Indian texts**, the mind is described as both *bandhu* (friend) and *shatru* (enemy). Left untamed, it lashes us with fear. Trained, it becomes the very ally that carries us forward.

- Buddhism often calls the mind a "monkey" — restless, chattering, sometimes cruel, but not evil. With practice, the monkey learns gentleness.
- Sufi mystics speak of the *nafs*, the ego-self, that scolds and shames in an effort to control us. Their remedy? Not suppression, but remembrance — returning again and again to compassion until the harshness softens.

Here's how I've come to see it: The critic is not your enemy. It is a badly programmed guru. It doesn't want you to fail, but it only knows one method: fear. It thinks that if it lashes you hard enough, you'll stay in line. It doesn't yet understand that kindness sustains far longer than cruelty.

And that's the invitation of this chapter. Not to exile the critic, but to retrain it. To teach it a new language. To let gratitude and compassion rewire its sentences until the voice that once shamed you begins — slowly — to guide you.

The Only Competition Worth Having

There's another habit the critic loves more than any other — **comparison.** It looks like motivation, but it quietly drains your peace.

You know, every time you compete with someone else, you're actually losing a piece of yourself. Because the moment you measure your worth against another person, you step away from your own soul.

Ancient wisdom has always warned us about this.

The **Bhagavad Gita** tells us: *"It is better to live your own path imperfectly than to live another's perfectly."* Competing with others drags us off our own path.

The **Buddha** taught that comparison is just another form of craving — and craving is the root of suffering.

Even **Marcus Aurelius**, centuries later, said: *"Waste no more time arguing about what a good man should be. Be one."*

They all point to the same truth: your only real competition is with yourself.

And modern science agrees. Psychologists call it **Social Comparison Theory** — the more we measure ourselves against others, the more anxious and unhappy we become. Why? Because there will always be someone with more money, more recognition, more "likes." That race never ends.

But here's the beautiful part: when you shift the question inward — *"Am I better than I was yesterday?"* — something powerful happens in the brain. **Neuroplasticity** kicks in: your brain literally rewires itself around growth, learning, and resilience. Studies in motivation psychology also show that true well-being doesn't come from competition, but from what's called **self-determination** — living with autonomy, competence, and purpose.

But here's the beautiful part: when you shift the question inward — when the critic says, *"They're ahead of you,"* the coach answers, *"But am I moving in the right direction?"* When the critic hisses, *"You'll never catch up,"* the coach replies, *"I'm not chasing them — I'm building me."* When the critic demands, *"Be better than them,"* the coach whispers, *"Be truer than yesterday."*

That's the quiet transformation: the scoreboard disappears. The race dissolves. The noise softens. And you begin to walk your own journey — steadily, peacefully, with integrity.

That's what your inner coach does — it stops keeping score against others and starts cheering for the person you're still becoming. And that shift, from comparison to compassion, is what finally allows the heart to rest.

When Gratitude Isn't Enough

By now, we've practiced gratitude — noticing the blanket, the tea, the breath still arriving each morning. And gratitude does change the weather inside. It steadies mood, shifts perspective, makes winter more livable.

But here's the paradox: even when you're being grateful, the critic doesn't retire. Sometimes it grows louder.

You whisper: *I'm grateful for this cup of tea.* The critic interrupts: *That's all? Shouldn't you be aiming higher?*

You write: *I'm grateful I showed up today.* The critic mutters: *But you missed yesterday. Doesn't that cancel it out?*

This is why gratitude alone cannot finish the work. The critic is clever; it knows how to sneak in through the very sentences meant to heal you. It weaponizes warmth, turning it into proof you're not grateful *enough.*

Science explains this trap. Negativity bias means the brain overweighs what's missing. Even when you list ten things you are grateful for, the critic zooms in on the one you forgot. Without self-compassion, gratitude becomes another checklist — and the critic loves checklists, because they always leave room for failure.

Here's the shift: gratitude names the gift, but self-compassion reminds you that you are worthy of receiving it. Without that worthiness, the critic keeps erasing progress.

This is not indulgence. It's fuel. Research from Kristin Neff and Chris Germer shows that self-compassion increases heart-rate variability (a measure of resilience). People who practice it are more motivated, not less — because kindness makes effort sustainable. When you believe you're allowed to fail and return, you keep showing up.

Spiritual traditions echo the same truth.

- In Zen, wandering is not failure; noticing is the practice. Each return is success.
- In the Hindu Philosophy, the mind is trained not by punishment but by steady return — abhyasa.

- In Sufism, the heart is polished not once, but endlessly, by remembering again and again.

So when the critic hijacks your gratitude, the answer isn't to abandon gratitude or to shout the critic down. The answer is to expand into self-compassion. Gratitude says: *I noticed this gift.* Self-compassion adds: *And I forgive myself for the times I missed it. I am still worthy of care.*

When you meet that critic with gratitude, and extend gratitude into kindness, you begin the re-programming. Gratitude says: *I noticed.* Kindness says: *I forgive myself.* Self-love says: *I still deserve care, even when I slip.*

This is the path from critic to coach. Not silencing the voice, but retraining it until it begins to sound more like an inner guide. This is how gratitude matures. It stops being a list of **thank-yous** to the world and becomes a practice of thank-you toward yourself — not for perfection, but for presence.

Completing the Circle

Gratitude, at first, seems simple: thank the blanket, the tea, the neighbor. But the hardest place to send it is inward. The critic doesn't let that pass easily. Even in gratitude it sneaks back:

- *"Yes, but you should have done more."*
- *"You're grateful now, but remember when you failed yesterday?"*
- *"Other people don't need to congratulate themselves for such small things."*

This is how the critic survives: by turning even warmth into another weapon. It convinces you that gratitude belongs everywhere but here, in your own chest. Yet if gratitude never turns inward, the circle is left open. You are thanking the world for its gifts but denying yourself the right to receive them. You are pouring warmth outward while keeping yourself in the cold.

Here is why gratitude must evolve into self-compassion. It is not enough to thank the world for its small mercies; you must thank yourself for noticing them. Not enough to be grateful for resilience; you must also be grateful to the part of you that kept showing up.

Self-compassion is not indulgence. It is strength turned inward. It is the quiet voice that says: *"I see you trying, even here, even now."*

Self-compassion is how the circle closes. It is gratitude applied inward — not for outcomes, but for effort. Not for perfection, but for presence.

- Gratitude says: *I am thankful this warmth exists.*
- Self-compassion says: *I am thankful I allowed myself to feel it.*

This distinction is everything. Without self-compassion, gratitude risks becoming performance — a list written in a notebook but never felt in the body. With self-compassion, gratitude becomes lived: you not only notice the gift but also soften enough to let it land.

Neuroscience confirms what the heart already knows: when you treat yourself with kindness, resilience strengthens, and habits endure. But beyond biology, there is something more spiritual here. Every tradition whispers it in its own language — that love which does not include yourself cannot last outward.

And so the practice needs to become circular: you thank the world, you thank yourself, you thank even the part of you that resisted, because resistance too is proof of care. Gratitude steadies the season; self-compassion steadies you inside it. Practice gentleness and kindness towards yourself, again and again, until return itself becomes habit.

Think of it like the seasons:

- Gratitude is spring's noticing — the crocus breaking through snow.
- Self-compassion is winter's patience — the soil that holds the seed even when no one sees it growing.

One without the other is incomplete. Gratitude without compassion becomes brittle. Compassion without gratitude becomes vague. Together, they form a cycle strong enough to hold you through setbacks.

And so the practice becomes circular:

- You thank the world.
- You thank yourself for noticing.
- You thank even the critic, in its clumsy way, for trying to keep you safe.

This is the true completion: not silencing the critic, but retraining it with kindness until it becomes your coach — the one who says, *You slipped, yes, but you returned. That's the real progress.*

Kindness in Action: A Flow of Stories

Kindness doesn't always arrive in sweeping gestures. More often, it shows itself in fragile, ordinary moments — when the critic could have taken over, but didn't.

Returning Instead of Quitting Take Anna, who had been consistent with her morning meditation for nearly three weeks. Then one Tuesday, she overslept. The critic pounced: *"See? You can't even keep a simple habit. You'll never change."* In the past, that sentence would have ended the ritual. She would have quit, convinced she had failed.

But this time, she paused. She placed her hand on her chest and wrote three lines in her journal:

- *I was kind enough to notice.*
- *I was kind enough to care that I slipped.*
- *I was kind enough to give myself another chance.*

That night she took the breaths of calm and sat for five minutes. It wasn't a flawless streak — but it was resilience wrapped in kindness. She didn't erase the slip; she softened it into a return.

Mira: Celebrating What the Critic Erases Mira's critic worked differently. It didn't attack her failures — it erased her progress. She journaled daily for two weeks, yet the voice sneered: *"It's nothing. Anyone could do that."* We reframed the practice: every milestone deserves kindness. She chose something small but symbolic — a chai latte from her favorite café every seventh day. At first, it felt indulgent. But after her first milestone, she told me: *"It felt like someone finally noticed me — and that someone was me."* Kindness here wasn't just for the ritual. It was for herself, for showing up, for refusing to let her progress vanish under dismissal.

Daniel: Standing Upright in the Storm Daniel faced not just an inner critic but an outer one. A clipped email from his manager spiraled into condemnation: *"You're failing. You're not good enough."* Instead of replaying the message endlessly, he opened his journal and wrote:

- *I am being kind to myself by admitting I care.*
- *I am being kind to myself by noticing how this hurt me.*
- *I am being kind to myself by choosing resilience instead of collapse.*

Later he told me: *"It didn't erase the sting. But it stopped me from turning against myself."* Kindness, in his case, wasn't denial — it was self-preservation.

My Own Winter Return I know this rhythm myself. One February, after weeks of keeping steady with my breathwork, I slipped back into old patterns — late-night scrolling, mornings heavy with fog. The critic arrived instantly: *"You call yourself a coach? You can't even live your own practices."* For a while, I believed it. Then, one night, I whispered into the dark: *"I am being kind to myself by starting again tomorrow."* That line was enough. The next morning I rose, not perfectly, but gently. The critic was still there, but kindness had the louder voice.'

A Larger Echo: The Phoenix in Winter These stories remind me of an ancient image — the phoenix. Legends say it burns, turns to ash, then rises again. But what we often forget is this: the ashes are not failure. They are the soil from which renewal comes. Kindness is what gathers the ash, holds it without judgment, and whispers: *"This, too, can be used."* The critic sees ashes as proof of collapse. Kindness sees ashes as preparation for flight.

Bridging Back to Practice Together, these moments — Anna's return, Mira's celebration, Daniel's resilience, my own faltering step — show us something essential: kindness is not about excusing failure. It is about making room to begin again. Winter habits are not sustained by punishment. They are sustained by return. And kindness is the hand on your back that helps you return gently, instead of scolding yourself into collapse.

> **Reflection Prompt:** Think of the last time you slipped from a habit – a meditation, a walk, a promise to yourself. Write down one sentence your critic used. Then rewrite it as an act of kindness: *"I slipped, and I am still allowed to begin again."* Notice how even that small shift changes the weather inside.

Why the Critic Is So Persistent

The critic survives because it is fast, sticky, and ancient. It has been rehearsing its lines for years, maybe decades, while kindness is often the newer voice in the room.

- **Negativity bias: The brain is Velcro for criticism and Teflon for praise.** Our ancestors remembered threats more than sunsets — survival depended on it. The critic still carries that wiring, scanning for danger even when the "threat" is just a missed journal entry. The brain is wired to remember criticism more vividly than praise. One harsh phrase — even from ourselves — can outweigh a dozen kind ones.
- **Neural grooves**: Each time we attack ourselves, we deepen the trench. *"You failed again"* becomes the default pathway, like water running into the same frozen groove each winter. Repeated self-criticism deepens pathways in the brain, making "failure" the default story.

- **The Stress loop**: Self-criticism spikes stress, narrowing our focus. Suddenly, all we can see is the misstep, while every bit of progress is hidden under snow.

Here's the part the critic doesn't understand: pressure is not the only way to survive. It thinks it is saving you by scolding. It believes vigilance keeps you safe. But evolution has moved forward — and your nervous system now thrives on something the critic never learned to trust: kindness.

Kindness interrupts the old loop. Each self-compassionate phrase lays a new track:

- *"I slipped — but I am still here."*
- *"I care enough to want better."*
- *"I am allowed to begin again."*

At first these tracks feel faint, like footprints in fresh snow. But repetition matters. Neuroscience calls it **neuroplasticity**— every time you choose kindness over criticism, you strengthen a new pathway. With enough practice, the brain begins to expect compassion instead of condemnation.

The critic's persistence, then, is not proof that you're broken. It is proof that your nervous system has been trained in one language for too long. Your work now is not to silence it, but to gently re-teach it. To let kindness become the louder voice, until the critic itself begins to soften and learn a new role: not accuser, but coach.

Reflection Prompt: Write down the sentence your critic repeats most often in winter. Now write its "kindness translation." Imagine you are retraining a well-meaning but clumsy guardian. What new words would you want it to learn?

Kindness as Self-Compassion in Disguise

At its core, kindness toward yourself is not indulgence — it is a form of self-compassion. And self-compassion is not softness that makes you weak. It is resilience disguised as gentleness.

Think of it as learning to treat yourself the way you would treat a friend you love:

- **Critic**: "You slipped again."
- **Coach**: "You noticed. That matters."
- **Critic**: "It's nothing."
- **Coach**: "It's something. You showed up, and that counts."
- **Critic**: "You'll never get this right."
- **Coach**: "You're learning. And learning always looks messy."

This is not about denying the critic's voice. It's about letting kindness have the last word.

Science backs this up. Research shows self-compassion lowers cortisol, increases emotional resilience, and builds persistence far more effectively than self-attack ever could. When you respond to yourself with warmth instead of judgment, your nervous system shifts into safety. Safe bodies try again. Unsafe ones shut down.

Spiritual Echoes of Return

Kindness is not a new invention. Every tradition that has weathered hardship has discovered some version of it — not as luxury, but as survival.

In **Zen practice**, the instruction is deceptively simple: *when the mind wanders, notice, and return.* There is no punishment for drifting. Wandering is expected. Returning is the point. Each act of coming back is seen not as weakness, but as strength.

In **yoga**, the principle of *abhyasa* — steady practice — teaches that discipline is not perfection, but persistence. You will fall out of postures. You will forget to breathe. But each time you return to the mat, even after weeks of absence, the practice welcomes you. Kindness makes that return possible.

In **Sufi mysticism**, the heart is said to be polished by *dhikr*, the remembrance of divine names. Forgetting is inevitable. Remembering again and again is what makes the heart shine. Each return is kindness extended inward — proof that you are still worthy of connection, even after distraction.

In **Christian mysticism**, there is the phrase: *love your neighbor as yourself.* The ordering matters. If love does not begin with yourself, it cannot expand outward with any strength. To return to kindness after failure is not selfishness; it is planting the root from which outward love grows.

Across traditions, the same rhythm emerges:

- Stray.
- Notice.
- Return.

The critic calls this cycle weakness. Wisdom calls it practice.

Kindness reframes the narrative. It reminds you that the stumble is not the end of the road — it is part of the road. What matters most is not that you fell, but that you cared enough to rise again.

Reflection Prompt: Write down one place in your life where you have "wandered" – a habit dropped, a practice forgotten, a ritual abandoned. Now write: *What would returning look like if I met myself with kindness instead of criticism?*

Practices to Weave Kindness into Your Winter

The critic is not silenced by argument. It quiets when you give it a new script — one written in warmth and repetition. These practices are not complicated. They are small doors you can walk through daily, until the voice of kindness feels as familiar as the critic once did.

1. Critic vs. Coach Rewrite

The critic thrives in repetition. To retrain it, you must give it new lines to repeat.

How to practice:

1. Write down three sentences your critic says most often.
   - "You failed again."
   - "This isn't enough."
   - "Why can't you get it right?"
2. Now rewrite them as a coach would:
   - "You noticed — and noticing means you're learning."
   - "This effort matters, even if it feels small."
   - "You're trying, and that's more than enough today."
3. Place these rewritten lines where you'll see them: a sticky note by your mirror, a card in your wallet, your phone's lock screen.

Why it works:

- The brain does not erase grooves of thought; it overlays them with new ones.
- Each rewrite is a rehearsal — carving a kinder path that becomes easier to walk over time.

> **Reflection Prompt: Tonight,** ask: *Which line did I hear more today – critic or coach? What can I do tomorrow to let the coach speak louder?*

2. The Hand-on-Heart Ritual

Kindness is not only verbal. It is physical. Your body responds to your own touch as it would to another's — releasing oxytocin, lowering stress, softening the nervous system.

How to practice:

1. Sit or stand somewhere quiet.
2. Place one hand over your heart, the other on your belly.
3. Take three slow breaths. On each exhale, whisper:
    - "I am safe in my own kindness."
    - "I am allowed to be human."
    - "I forgive myself for today."
4. Pause. Let the warmth of your hand anchor the words into your body.

Why it works:

- Touch activates the parasympathetic nervous system.
- Breath pairs words with sensation, making them believable.
- Spiritual traditions — from yogic mudras to Christian crossing to Sufi hand-over-heart prayer — have long known the power of hand-to-heart gestures.

> **Reflection Prompt: After** this ritual, write one phrase that felt true in your body. Keep it somewhere visible to return to when the critic shouts loudest.

3. Kindness Log for Slips

Most journals track success. But the critic thrives in the dark corners where we stumble. This practice reframes slips as opportunities for kindness.

How to practice:

1. Each evening, instead of only recording what went "well," add one line:
   - "I'm grateful I noticed my slip."
   - "I allowed myself to rest instead of forcing."
   - "I cared enough to feel disappointed."
2. Over weeks, the log becomes proof that slipping is not the opposite of progress — it is the soil where compassion grows.

Why it works:

- Repetition trains the Reticular Activating System (RAS) to notice not just mistakes, but recoveries.
- You slowly begin to see yourself not as the one who fails, but as the one who returns.

4. Milestone Ritual – Celebrating Small Wins

The critic loves to erase progress. Celebration is how you remind yourself that each step matters.

How to practice:

1. Choose one habit you want to strengthen (journaling, walking, breathwork).
2. Pick a milestone: 7 days, 14 days, 21 days.
3. Decide how you will celebrate when you arrive:
   - A favorite warm drink.
   - A small gift to yourself.
   - Simply saying aloud: *"I kept my promise to myself."*

Why it works:

- Neuroscience shows the dopamine reward system cements behaviors.
- Spiritually, rituals of marking time (Sabbath, festivals, feast days) have always reinforced resilience and meaning.

> **Reflection Prompt:** Ask: *What celebration feels kind, not performative? What gift would remind me that showing up matters?*

5. The Three Kindnesses Before Bed

A simple ritual to end the day in warmth instead of criticism.

How to practice:
Each night, write down three things directed inward:

1. One thing I'm kind to myself for noticing.
2. One thing I'm kind to myself for trying.
3. One thing I'm kind to myself for allowing (rest, laughter, pause).

Why it works:

- Redirects the mind from replaying failures to rehearsing care.
- Sets the nervous system into a softer state for sleep.
- Over time, rewires identity: you stop being "the one who failed" and become "the one who always returns with kindness."

"The critic says you failed. The coach whispers: you returned – and that is enough."

Closing Reflection

The critic will not vanish overnight. It will still knock at your door in winter's silence — reminding you of slips, dismissing your progress, **comparing you with others**, questioning your worth. But now you have something it cannot undo: the choice to meet yourself with kindness.

Each practice — whether a line rewritten, a hand on your heart, or a small celebration — is not about silencing the critic; it's about softening its voice until it learns new words. Slowly, the harsh taskmaster becomes a quieter guide. Slowly, vigilance gives way to encouragement.

This is not indulgence. It is fuel — the kind that makes habits sustainable and resilience enduring.

So tonight, before sleep, place a hand on your heart. Whisper one sentence of kindness to yourself. Notice how your body shifts when you allow the gentler voice to speak. That shift — small, ordinary, invisible to anyone else — is how winters are transformed.

Because in the end, growth is not measured by never stumbling. It is measured by becoming the one who stumbles, notices, and returns — again and again, with kindness.

"Kindness is not the absence of the critic – it is the presence of a gentler voice that teaches you how to return."

CHAPTER SEVEN SUMMARY - FROM INNER CRITIC TO INNER COACH

Key Insight

The inner critic is not an enemy – it's an outdated guardian still using fear as its language. Self-compassion retrains it into an ally. When you replace self-attack with warmth, cortisol drops, oxytocin rises, and resilience strengthens. Kindness becomes the quiet fuel that makes progress sustainable.

Core Metaphors

- The Badly Programmed Guru: The critic means well but teaches through fear; compassion updates its method.
- Walls into Doorways: Gratitude softens the critic's edge; self-compassion completes the circle by turning judgment into return.
- The Phoenix in Winter: Kindness gathers the ashes of failure and turns them into soil for renewal.

Practices for Self-Compassion

- Critic-to-Coach Rewrite – Replace recurring self-attacks with compassionate translations; post them where you'll see them daily.
- Hand-on-Heart Ritual – Pair gentle touch and breath with forgiveness phrases to anchor safety in the body.
- Kindness Log for Slips – Record not only successes but moments you noticed and returned.
- Milestone Ritual – Celebrate small continuities; let dopamine and meaning reinforce the habit.
- Three Kindnesses Before Bed – End each day naming three inward kindnesses: noticing, trying, allowing.

Reflection Prompts

- What phrase does my critic repeat most often? What is its kindness translation?
- When did I last slip, and how can I meet that moment with gentleness instead of blame?
- What celebration feels kind, not performative – one that reminds me that showing up matters?

Closing Meditation Mantras

"The critic says you failed. The coach whispers: you returned – and that is enough."

"I am retraining my inner voice – from critic to coach, from scolding to guiding, from fear to kindness."

PART II

Ready Companions

CHAPTER EIGHT

The Loneliness, Growing Your Light & Pruning What Drains It

(learning to enjoy your own company, build healthy connection, and gently set boundaries with what diminishes you)

The first garden you will ever tend is your own presence. Grow what nourishes you, and prune what steals the sun

Leaning into the Ache

There are two kinds of winter quiet.

One feels sacred — snow drifting against the window, the steady hum of a heater, the whole world pausing to breathe with you. In that hush, you can feel your shoulders drop, your pulse steady. This quiet is medicine. It invites you to listen, to rest, to return to yourself.

And then there's the other kind of quiet — the one that presses down. The evenings that stretch too long. The canceled plans. The empty chair at the table. The weekends when everyone else seems gathered elsewhere while you refresh your phone for a message that never comes. This quiet is heavy; it drags. It can follow you even into crowded rooms — a family dinner where you feel unseen, an office where you feel replaceable.

When I first moved to Canada, I met this second kind of quiet. Everything felt both promising and fragile. Within months of arriving, a slipped disc forced me to leave the job I'd waited half a year to begin. My body ached, my circle was small, and the nights seemed endless. Snow piled high outside while silence filled the space within.

That season became my teacher. I had no network to lean on, so I leaned inward. I named the ache — not with words, but with presence. I stopped turning away from it and listened. I sat with my breath until it steadied. I wrote small affirmations on scraps of paper and taped them to the wall, so they'd greet me each morning. Slowly, those practices became my companions. They didn't melt the snow outside, but they kept the hearth within alive

One of those affirmations was about love — a quiet declaration that I was ready for connection, even when nothing in my life looked ready for it. And in the middle of that winter, still without work and with only a few acquaintances, I met the woman who would become my wife. The season hadn't changed, but my inner climate had.

We all have a season like that — when the world outside feels frozen, and the one within begins to thaw.

The capacity to soothe yourself, to stay gentle with your own presence, becomes a companion through every season of change.

Reflection Prompt: Think of a time you felt truly alone. What small act – a breath, a phrase, a gentle ritual – helped you through? If nothing helped then, what could you offer yourself now, in retrospect?

Learning to Enjoy Your Own Company

Loneliness is not weakness. It's a signal — an invitation to meet yourself kindly. It asks: *Can you tend your own fire while you wait for the circle to form?* When you learn to make your own company a place you want to inhabit, you discover a lifelong skill: how to create inner warmth when the world feels cold.

It may feel uneasy at first to be with yourself. It's not just a winter thing. It can happen on a bright afternoon when plans fall through, in a hotel room after a conference, even in a crowded party where you suddenly feel invisible.

Most of us have been trained to reach outward in those moments — to fill the space with noise, scrolling, food, or busyness. We've learned to escape ourselves. But there's another path: learning to make your own company pleasant. Not as a replacement for people, but as a foundation for how you meet them.

The ancient texts of yoga and the Upanishads understood this. They called it *antar-mouna* — inner silence. The practice of sitting quietly, not to withdraw from the world, but to befriend the mind. In classical yoga, the first steps are not postures, but principles: yamas (ethical foundations) and niyamas (personal observances) — *svadhyaya* (self-study) and *santosha* (contentment). These are ways of becoming at ease in your own presence.

Across spiritual traditions, the first discovery is always self-discovery; the first relationship is with oneself. The breathing and meditation practices you met earlier come from this same lineage — tools to steady your inner climate so that when you step outward, you bring calm with you.

Learning to enjoy your own company is not isolation — it's mastery. In yogic language, it is swaraj, self-rule in its truest form. When you are comfortable in your own presence, you stop clinging to draining people, stop performing for approval, stop mistaking noise for connection. You bring a quieter confidence to everything — your work, your relationships, your choices.

When you become someone you like being alone with, your calm travels with you — on a winter commute, at a summer gathering, or sitting quietly in an empty room.

When you can sit with yourself in peace, even winter begins to feel like home.

> **Reflection Prompt:** Recall a time you felt uneasy in your own company. What might have changed if, instead of reaching outward, you had offered yourself one small act of kindness – a breath, a word, or a ritual?

Connection Without Clinging

When you have learned to sit kindly with yourself, connection stops being a way to escape loneliness and becomes a way to enrich life. You no longer reach out from emptiness; you reach out from steadiness. It stops being a desperate grab and becomes a deliberate reaching out. Instead of clinging to people to quiet your discomfort, you invite them to share the steadiness you've built inside. That shift is what makes belonging nourishing rather than draining.

Cultures that live with long dark seasons have always understood this. In Scandinavia, people don't wait for perfect circumstances to gather; they build rituals of connection into everyday life. Fika in Sweden — a pause for coffee and something sweet — is not just about caffeine. It's a daily act of softening isolation, of saying "let's be human together" in the middle of work. In Norway, friends meet for *friluftsliv* — open-air living — even in January. Walks under frozen trees, a thermos passed between hands, conversation or silence as needed. These small, reliable rituals become a second layer of warmth over each person's inner fire.

But you don't have to live in Scandinavia to practice this. Connection doesn't need to be elaborate. It might be one text to a friend saying, "thinking of you," a ten-minute call, a walk around the block with a neighbor, or inviting someone over for soup. What matters is that it's a conscious act — an offering rather than a plea.

When connection is approached this way, it multiplies what you already have. Breath steadies you from the inside; a shared breath in laughter steadies you from the outside. Gratitude shifts your perspective; shared gratitude amplifies it. Compassion softens your critic; being with others reminds you you're not the only one carrying one.

This is why we build inner practices first: so that when you reach out, you're not handing someone your emptiness and asking them to fill it. You're sharing your warmth. And when the circle gathers — whether it's two people or twenty — the night feels shorter, the cold less harsh, no matter the season.

Reflection Prompt: Think of one simple, pressure-free way you could invite someone into your life this week – a coffee, a walk, a call. How does it feel different when you approach it as a sharing of steadiness rather than a reach for rescue?

Mapping Your Support Circle

Even when you've learned to enjoy your own company and to reach out without clinging, the critic may still whisper, "You have no one. Don't bother reaching out. You're on your own." That's rarely true. More often, we've simply forgotten the variety of support already around us. Even when your inner world feels grey, there are usually threads of connection waiting to be noticed.

One practice I give clients is to map a support circle of five people — not just names but roles. Thinking in roles rather than names frees you from the idea that one perfect person has to meet all your needs. It also frees you from the belief that you *must* have a big circle. It's perfectly okay if your mosaic is small — even one or two people playing more than one role can be enough. What matters is quality, not quantity.

Here's a simple template:

- **The Listener** — the one who hears you without trying to fix.
- **The Laugher** — the one who cracks a joke and breaks the heaviness.
- **The Companion** — the one who will simply walk beside you, in silence if needed.
- **The Mentor** — the one who steadies you with perspective.
- **The Coach** — the one who keeps you accountable, reminding you of your own strength.

When you see your circle labelled this way, you realise you don't need one perfect person. You need a mosaic — even a small, imperfect one. Some days you'll need laughter. Other days, grounding. Other days, a gentle push. Knowing who to call for what breaks the illusion that you're "too much" or "asking too much." It also reminds you that connection is not about clinging — it's about balance.

Reflection Prompt: Write down your five roles and fill in names beside them. Notice which roles are strong, which are missing, and which might be filled by someone new. Keep the list somewhere visible as a reminder: *Connection strengthens me; it does not define me.*

De-seeding Drainers: Pruning With Kindness

In the last section you mapped your support circle — the Listener, the Laugher, the Companion, the Mentor, the Coach — and began to see your relationships as a mosaic rather than a single lifeline. That mosaic is a powerful tool because it shows you the variety of nourishment already around you.

But a mosaic also reveals its cracks. As soon as you lay out your tiles, you may notice a few that don't belong — interactions that leave you tense, doubting yourself, or feeling smaller than when you arrived. This is the other side of connection. It's what the critic feeds on when it whispers: *"You're too much. You ask for too much. Everyone else copes, so why can't you?"*

Connection matters. But not all company is gentle. De-seeding is the process of recognising which people or patterns in your life repeatedly dim your light, whether through doubt, negativity, or emotional wear. It isn't about cutting everyone off; it's about pruning out what no longer serves the garden of your soul so the healthy parts can thrive.

Recognising the Drainers

Based on patterns I've seen in clients and reflected in wellness psychology, some relationship roles can quietly erode your energy if you're not aware of them. They often don't look like villains; they can be friends, colleagues, even family. Seeing the pattern isn't about hate or judgement. It's about clarity, so you can decide how to protect your light.

- **The Doubter** — This is the person who, often without malice, plants tiny seeds of uncertainty in your mind. You tell them about a dream or a goal, and their first response is "Are you sure you're good enough?" or "That sounds risky…" Over time their questions can sound like concern but feel like cold water on your enthusiasm. One client told me she could predict the Doubter's eyebrow raise before she even spoke; she started sharing less and doubting herself more.

- **The Belittler** — Someone who diminishes your feelings or efforts, usually under the guise of "helping" or "being honest." You open up about a challenge, and they say, "Oh, that's nothing, you're overreacting" or "Everyone does that, why are you making it a big deal?" This steady minimising can make you feel small, even when you're trying your best. It's not always intentional, but it chips away at self-trust.
- **The Energy Vampire** — This person always needs something — advice, reassurance, a listening ear — but rarely gives back. You leave conversations feeling wrung out and guilty for wanting space. They might call in crisis after crisis, and at first you feel noble helping, but eventually you notice your own tank running dry. Energy Vampires aren't necessarily bad people; they're just chronically pulling instead of reciprocating.
- **The One-Upper** — You share a story about your weekend run, and they immediately tell you about their marathon. You mention a stressful week at work, and they recount how theirs was even worse. Every experience becomes a competition in which you're always one step behind. It seems harmless, but over time it trains you to downplay your joy and your struggles alike because everything gets eclipsed.
- **The Gossip Carrier / Critic** — This is the person whose conversations revolve around other people's flaws, failures, and scandals. You might think you're bonding, but you leave feeling slimy or low. Their constant criticism becomes a soundtrack in your head, making you more negative by proximity. Even if they never criticize you directly, being in their orbit normalises a climate of judgement.
- **The Narcissist** — The person who acts like they are the centre of the universe, always right, the best at everything — and isn't afraid to tell you so. No matter how smart or experienced you are, you can never quite measure up. They may charm you at first, but over time their need for admiration and lack of empathy erodes confidence and self-trust. With a narcissist, you often find yourself questioning your reality, apologising for things that weren't your fault, or shrinking to avoid their disapproval.

Recognising these archetypes is not about labelling people for hate; it's about clarity. When you can name a pattern, you can decide what to share, what to limit, and where to place your energy. Clarity creates choice, and choice creates freedom.

When the Pattern Has a Name: Jennifer's Story

Jennifer was a mid-level project manager in a large tech company. By the time she reached out to me, she wasn't burned out in the classic sense — she still exercised, kept up her gratitude journal, and meditated most mornings — but she described a constant low-level exhaustion and second-guessing herself. "I'm doing all the right things," she said, "but I feel like my confidence is leaking out somewhere."

As we unpacked her week, a pattern emerged. Jennifer had a close university friend she still spoke with almost daily. The friend had been a steady presence through break-ups and job changes. Yet Jennifer noticed that after each conversation she felt smaller. If she mentioned a new idea at work, the friend would say, "That's risky; people might not like it." If Jennifer shared excitement about a certification she was studying for, the friend would warn, "Be careful — it's really tough. You're already overloaded." The tone was always framed as caring. But the effect was predictable: Jennifer's enthusiasm dimmed and her self-doubt spiked.

When we mapped her support circle — Listener, Laugher, Companion, Mentor, Coach — she realised she had automatically listed this friend under "Listener." Seeing it on paper, she admitted the actual role was closer to "Doubter." That single reframing allowed Jennifer to stop making herself wrong. She didn't have to villainise her friend, but she could stop handing over her most vulnerable ideas to someone who reflexively poked holes in them.

Jennifer began with small, concrete changes. She shifted their calls to twice a week and kept them short. She stopped sharing early-stage dreams with that friend and instead discussed them with a supportive mentor at work. She added a "Laugher" to her circle — a coworker she took quick walking breaks with at lunch. Within six weeks Jennifer reported that her inner chatter had calmed. "I still like my friend," she said, "but I don't leave the phone call feeling like I've been talked out of myself." Her meditation and affirmations felt effective again because she wasn't pouring them into a sieve.

Pruning with Kindness: Practical Steps

Someone once said, *"The easiest way to failure is trying to please everyone."* The point isn't to hate or discard people; it's to protect your mental well-being. Remember: you are not everyone, and everyone is not for you. People may be right in their own way, but if their way doesn't work for you, you have the right to choose different company — or simply less of theirs. Pruning is tending the ecosystem of your life so your inner steadiness has room to root.

Boundaries don't have to be dramatic. More often they're small, consistent shifts that quietly reclaim your energy. Here are some ways to "de-seed" draining patterns while keeping compassion:

1. **Notice the after-effect.** Pay attention to how you feel after interactions. Uplifted? Drained? Tense? Calm? This is your nervous system giving you data, not judgement.
2. **Name the role.** In your journal or mind, name the behaviour you're experiencing ("Doubter," "Belittler," "Narcissist") rather than a label like "bad friend." This keeps you objective and allows for nuance.
3. **Adjust what you share.** You may not need to cut someone off. Often the first step is to stop offering them your most tender material — your dreams, your insecurities. Share those with people who can hold them without poking holes.
4. **Limit exposure where you can.** If the person is a friend or acquaintance, you might reduce the frequency or duration of contact or change the

setting (a quick coffee instead of a long dinner). Replace some of that time with people or activities that fill you.

5. **Navigate unavoidable relationships.** Some people — bosses, relatives, key colleagues — may be impossible to avoid entirely. In these cases, boundaries can look like internal scripts ("That's their fear, not my truth"), keeping conversations to neutral topics, or scheduling a brief reset (a walk, a breath, a supportive text) immediately after the interaction to clear their energy from yours.
6. **Use gentle language.** If a direct boundary is needed, frame it kindly: "I'm working on protecting my focus right now, so I won't be discussing that project in detail." Boundaries can be clear without being cruel.
7. **Fill the space intentionally.** When you prune, don't leave a vacuum. Invite in nourishing company, new rituals, or simply more time in your own pleasant self-company. Space itself can be healing if you fill it with light.

Boundaries aren't about rejection; they're about your respect — for your growth, your light, and your becoming. You don't need perfect relationships. You need honest ones. And sometimes self-company is better than forced company until the right circle forms.

> **Reflection Prompt:** Think of one person or interaction in your life that leaves you consistently drained. What is one gentle boundary or adjustment you could make this week to protect your energy – and what could you fill that space with instead?

Companionship & Carrying Light Forward

You've learned to sit kindly with yourself. You've learned to reach out without clinging, to map your circle, and to prune what drains you. In doing so you've created something rare: a foundation of inner steadiness and an outer network that mirrors it back to you.

Companionship, at its healthiest, isn't a rescue; it's a resonance. It's two steady flames making a room brighter, not one flame keeping the other alive. Whether that companionship comes from a mentor, a friend, a walk with a neighbour, or a coach, it grows best when you already know how to be at ease in your own presence. That is the true power of the work you've been doing: it makes you a better companion to yourself and a better companion to others.

Of course, when you begin to set boundaries or step back from draining relationships, a vacuum can appear. That empty space isn't a failure; it's an opening. In the next chapter we'll turn toward filling that space deliberately — creating your own "Happy List" of practices, people, places and small joys that nourish you. This is how you stack your inner firewood before the next storm and ensure that whenever life narrows, you have warmth ready at hand.

Take a moment now to notice the shift. You're no longer waiting for someone else to change the weather for you. You're tending your own hearth and inviting companions who bring their own sparks. That's how you move from surviving winters — outer or inner — to shaping a life that feels steady, connected and alive in every season.

Reflection Prompt: Looking at the spaces you've created by setting boundaries, what is one small joy, ritual, or person you'd like to invite in next? Write it down as a seed for your "Happy List."

CHAPTER EIGHT SUMMARY - LONELINESS, GROWING YOUR LIGHT & PRUNING WHAT DRAINS IT

Key Insight

Loneliness isn't weakness; it's a signal. It asks you to tend your own inner fire while you wait for the circle to form. When you learn to enjoy your own company, you stop clinging to draining people just to avoid being alone, and connection shifts from escape to enrichment. Pruning relationships with kindness creates space for balanced companionship and for your own calm to travel with you everywhere.

Core Metaphors

- First Garden - Your presence is the first soil you tend; grow what nourishes, prune what steals the sun.
- Inner Fire in Winter - External seasons may stay cold, but you can light a steady inner flame.
- Mosaic, Not One Lifeline - Support doesn't have to be one perfect person; even a small mosaic of roles can sustain you.
- Pruning With Kindness - Boundaries aren't rejection; they're respect for your growth and self-respect.

Practices for Self-Company & Balanced Connection

- Inner Silence Sit - A few minutes of antar-mouna (inner silence) or breath after waking, before screens, to polish the mirror of the mind.
- Map Your Support Circle - List five roles (Listener, Laugher, Companion, Mentor, Coach). Fill with names; even one or two people playing multiple roles is enough.

- Connection Without Clinging - Choose one conscious outreach this week (a call, a walk, a text) as an offering, not a plea.
- Pruning with Kindness - Notice the after-effect of interactions; adjust what you share; limit exposure or create internal scripts with unavoidable people.
- Fill the Space Intentionally - Replace time spent with draining people by inviting in nourishing company, new rituals, or pleasant self-company.

Reflection Prompts

- Think of a time you felt truly alone. What small act helped you get through? If nothing helped then, what could you offer yourself now?
- Identify one draining interaction. What is one gentle boundary you could set this week, and what would you like to fill that space with instead?

Closing Meditation Mantra

"I tend my own garden of presence. I grow what nourishes me. I prune with kindness what steals the sun. I carry my light with me in every season."

CHAPTER NINE

The Happy List: Your Personal Winter Medicine Cabinet

Calm isn't something we travel to find. It's something we build, moment by moment, right where we are.

Prelude – From Escape to Enrichment: Your Sacred Responsibility

All through this book you've been quietly building an inner architecture:

- acceptance, so winter no longer feels like punishment;
- openness, so light can return in drops;
- food for body and mind, so you stay steady instead of scattered;
- breath and meditation, so you can anchor instead of drift;
- affirmations, gratitude and self-kindness, so the critic softens and the coach emerges.

Those were your roots. This chapter is about your branches — the small, deliberate joys that grow out of that foundation and keep you nourished day by day.

Think of it as your sacred responsibility to yourself. When you tend to your own steadiness, you're not taking time away from your roles; you're fuelling them. A calm nervous system makes you a clearer leader, a kinder parent, a steadier friend. This is the place in the book where you stop only "practising" calm and start stocking it—like wood piled beside the stove before a storm.

And you don't need an hour or a perfect setting — only a few intentional moments that bring you back to yourself. Science shows that even two to five minutes of a chosen joy—music, a walk to your haven, a mindful sip of tea— can raise dopamine and oxytocin and widen perspective. These are micro-rituals, not chores. They're your quick-reach medicine.

Fika & Kakkukahvi: Pauses That Taste Like Light

Because winter — outer or inner — narrows our worlds. Daylight shrinks, routines constrict, choices feel fewer, and old habits creep back. That's exactly when a Happy List matters.

In Sweden they call it fika; in Finland, kakkukahvi. On the surface it's coffee and cake, but underneath it's a practice: stop, warm your hands around a mug, break bread or a bun, and share a few unhurried minutes with someone. It's not about caffeine or sugar; it's about presence. In dark months, rituals like these knit connection back into the day.

You don't have to be in Stockholm or Helsinki to practice it. A cup of tea or coffee, a slice of something you like, five minutes with a friend or by yourself can become your own fika. These are the kinds of micro-rituals your Happy List should hold — quick-reach medicine you stock beside the stove before a storm.

Building Your Happy List

Your Happy List is not self-care as marketed. It is not an algorithm's carousel of "30 hacks to feel better." It is not a mood board of other people's pleasures.

It is a slow, honest inventory of what genuinely steadies you — music, shows, rituals, places, and objects chosen by your own hands, from your own life. A cabinet you build yourself: music that truly lifts you, shows that genuinely soothe you, rituals that whisper "I'm safe," places where your breath deepens. Your list is not an escape. It's your personal method of staying connected to life when life feels heavy.

And if you slip—if you forget, scroll, binge, or skip—remember this isn't failure; it's exactly why you're stocking your Happy List. You're building a handrail for the days you wobble, not a checklist to get perfect. These micro-joys are meant to be ready when you are, especially on the days when energy or willpower feel thin.

But here's the secret: you don't always need to *add* something new. Often the gentlest reset is hidden inside what you're already doing. Your shower, your coffee, your walk to the mailbox, even the doorway you pass through on your way to work—each one is an unclaimed pause, a small doorway back to calm.

That's why the next section isn't another list of "extra" practices. It's a guide to waking up inside the ones you already have. These five tiny mindfulness practices transform everyday actions into stealth rituals, like sips of calm between bigger rituals, keeping your nervous system steady all day.

> *"Your Happy List is not a borrowed mood board. It's the living branch that grows from everything you've planted–micro-joys stacked before the storm, chosen by your own hands."*

5 Tiny Mindfulness Practices for Mundane Moments

Sometimes the simplest way to steady yourself isn't to add a new ritual, but to wake up inside the ones you already do. We brush, shower, eat, and walk on autopilot — and with them, we miss dozens of built-in chances to reset. In the context of this book, these small pauses are your stealth practices. They're like sips of calm between bigger rituals, keeping your nervous system steady all day.

Bringing presence to these everyday acts turns the ordinary into medicine. You don't need extra time, special cushions, or a perfect space. You only need to notice things like water hitting your skin, your feet meeting the floor, the texture of food on your tongue, the sound of your own breath. Each moment is already here; mindfulness lets it become a micro-practice of grounding and renewal.

1. **The Shower Pause** Before you reach for the soap, pause for one extra minute. Feel the water droplets hit your scalp. Trace their path down your shoulders. Listen to the sound. Inhale the steam as if it were a forest. *Why it works:* Warm water plus slow attention signals safety to the nervous system, and anchors you in the body.

2. **The Mindful Toothbrush** As you brush, put your phone away. Notice the taste of the paste, the movement of the bristles, the way your mouth feels clean. Breathe through your nose while you do it. *Why it works:* Pairing a twice-daily habit with sensory awareness builds mindfulness without extra time.

3. **The First Sip Ritual** Before coffee or tea disappears on autopilot, hold the cup in both hands. Notice its warmth. Inhale its scent. Take your first sip slowly, feeling it travel down. *Why it works:* Warmth in the hands and conscious sipping can help activate the vagus nerve, which is associated with calming the stress response

4. **The Slow Bite** At one meal a day, take the first three bites in silence. Notice texture, temperature, and flavour. Chew slowly. Feel gratitude for what you're eating before moving on. *Why it works:* Slowing the first bites helps prime digestion, steady blood sugar, and shifts you from "fight/flight" to "rest/digest."

5. **The Threshold Breath** Each time you cross a doorway — into a room, out of your house, into your car — use it as a cue. One slow inhale, one slow exhale. Imagine leaving behind what you don't need in the old space. *Why it works:* Associating a breath with a doorway creates micro-pauses throughout your day, lowering accumulated tension.

These five tiny mindfulness practices show you how to harvest calm from the everyday — a pause hidden in your shower, a breath at the doorway, a slower first sip of tea. They're like stealth refills for your inner reservoir, requiring no extra time, only new attention.

And yet, there will still be days when even these micro-pauses feel out of reach — when your mind is too loud, your body too tired, and you need something that reaches you before you can reach it. The body still knows how to return to calm — through sound, story, ritual, place, and touch.

I call these the five medicines of winter:

- Music that moves you.
- Stories that soothe you.
- Rituals that warm you.
- Places that lift you.
- And an emergency drawer of reminders for when you forget them all.

Each one is a different path to steadiness — proof that healing doesn't come from effort alone. Sometimes, it comes from allowing the small, ordinary things to do their quiet work.

1. Music as Medicine

When winter — outer or inner — presses hardest, sometimes meditation feels too far away, journaling feels like work, and gratitude feels forced. But music—music is simple. It travels faster than thought. You don't have to "do" it; you only have to let it in.

I've watched this play out again and again. One client, a lawyer who dreaded January mornings, told me: "I didn't fight it. I played my song. By the second verse, my body was already moving." Another, recovering from heartbreak, kept one song on repeat every night before sleep. "It's like the song holds me," she said.

Why it works:

- **Biology:** Upbeat rhythms increase dopamine, lifting mood. Calming melodies are associated with increased serotonin and reduced anxiety. Familiar songs light up oxytocin, giving you the same warmth as human connection.
- **Psychology:** When life feels unpredictable, knowing the next note gives your nervous system a sense of safety. Predictability is a soothing balm.
- **Spirit:** Music is one of humanity's oldest medicines — drums under Arctic skies, chants in temples, songs by fires. Every culture uses rhythm to steady hearts.

And here's the key: your winter playlist should be **yours**. Not the one Spotify suggests. Not the viral "calm vibes" loop from Instagram. This is about sound that you have lived with or want to live into — songs that have held you before, or that whisper possibility now.

Think of your playlist as medicine, not background noise. Like herbs in a jar, each song has its own effect. Build it the way healers once mixed balms: with intention.

Reflection Prompt: My Winter Playlist –

- Three songs that lift me when I feel heavy.
- Three songs that calm me when I feel scattered.
- Three songs that comfort me when I feel alone.

Write them down. Keep them where you can see them. Just looking at the list can shift your state, because anticipation itself releases dopamine. It is a small act of stacking firewood before the storm

"Your winter playlist isn't a trend. It's a medicine mixed from sound – chosen by your own hands, for your own heart."

2. Comfort-Watching as Anchoring

Not every tool on your Happy List needs to be lofty. Some are humble, even ordinary. Comfort-watching often gets a bad reputation — "shouldn't I be doing something better with my time?" — but when chosen with intention, it is one of the simplest ways to regulate a stressed nervous system in winter.

Think of it this way: when life feels unpredictable, predictability itself becomes medicine. Knowing the joke before it lands, anticipating the ending, recognizing the characters — all of that signal to your body: **you are safe here**. Your heart rate slows. Your breath softens.

I learned this during my winter of back pain. Sitcoms weren't distraction; they were anchors. They gave me something reliable when my body and mind felt unpredictable. A client of mine keeps a small rotation of "old favourites" just for heavy evenings. Another has a single film she watches every December to remind herself that warmth returns.

Why it works:

- **Biology:** Familiar storylines help steady the heart rate — like rocking a baby with a known lullaby.
- **Psychology:** Predictable narratives offer control when everything else feels uncertain.
- **Spirit:** Storytelling has always been a winter survival tool. Long before streaming, families gathered by firelight to tell the same tales again and again. Repetition wasn't boredom; it was belonging.

And just like the music section, this isn't about scrolling whatever the algorithm throws at you. It's about **choosing consciously**. What story helps you rest right now? Which characters feel like companions rather than noise?

> **Reflection Prompt: My Comfort-Watch List** - Three shows or films that always make me laugh. - Three that calm me when I'm scattered. - one I'll revisit this winter with intention.

Write them down. Keep the list somewhere visible. When a hard day hits, you won't have to think — you'll have a gentle anchor ready.

"Familiar stories aren't laziness.
They're firelight for the mind – warmth you can
return to when nights feel long."

3. Joy Rituals That Warm the Day

Not every item on your Happy List needs to come from a screen. Some of the most potent medicine sits quietly in the ordinary moments of a day. In winter — and in the "winters" of our lives — small rituals become lifelines. They tell your nervous system, *I am cared for. I am safe.*

Long before streaming or playlists, people used ritual as warmth. Lighting a lamp at dusk. Pouring tea for a guest. Stirring a pot that had been simmering all afternoon. These weren't just tasks; they were signals to the body: slow down, anchor here.

Today, you can reclaim that instinct. A ritual doesn't have to be elaborate or Instagram-worthy. It just needs to be something you return to with intention, something that marks a pause between the rush of hours.

Here are a few examples my clients have built into their Happy Lists:

- Always do small meditations, like 4-2-6 breathing or a smile meditation before journaling — small acts to turn writing from a chore into a mindful practice.
- Taking a hot bath with eucalyptus oil after a long commute — a reset for muscles and mood.
- Holding a mug of tea until your fingers thaw and your breath slows — simple warmth, but powerful grounding.
- Cooking a dish that makes your home smell like childhood — scent as memory, memory as medicine.

Why it works:

- **Biology:** Repetitive, soothing actions can lower heart rate. Warmth and scent activate the parasympathetic nervous system, moving the body out of fight-or-flight.
- **Psychology:** Ritual creates predictability in a season that feels unpredictable. It tells your mind: here is a safe space.
- **Spirit:** Across cultures, ritual is the bridge between ordinary time and sacred time. Even a small ritual whispers, *this moment matters.*

And just like music or comfort-watching, these rituals are not about what an influencer does or what looks pretty online. They're about what *you* do — tiny, authentic gestures that your body will begin to recognize as home.

Reflection Prompt: My Winter Joy Rituals

Write three simple rituals that warm your day. They can be from the list above or your own. Keep them visible. When heaviness hits, you won't have to invent self-care – you'll already have a pattern ready to step into.

"A ritual is a small door you open every day to let warmth in."

4. Places That Lift You

Winter — or any personal winter — shrinks geography. Home, work, commute. Repeat. The narrowing itself can become suffocating. When our world contracts, our nervous system reads it as danger: *no options, no exits.* That's why one of the most healing things you can do is name the places that lift you — the spaces that make your body exhale the moment you walk in.

Long before we had apps or "self-care," people had places of refuge. A kitchen table lit by a lamp. A library corner. A winter trail cut through the woods. Sacred spots weren't always churches or temples; they were any place where the nervous system knew: *I can breathe here.*

Your Happy List needs these spaces. They don't have to be far away, expensive, or photogenic. They just have to be yours — chosen for how they make you feel, not for how they might look on someone else's feed.

Here's how one client built what she called her "Sanctuary Map":

- Three indoor places: a café with big windows, a particular chair in her apartment, a quiet alcove in her local library.
- Three outdoor places: a short winter trail near home, a park bench she could reach in five minutes, her own balcony where she could wrap in a blanket and look at the sky. She taped the list to her fridge. On heavy days she didn't debate what to do — she picked a sanctuary and went.

Why it works:

- **Biology:** New or nurturing environments release dopamine, especially when paired with movement.
- **Psychology:** Having a ready-made list interrupts decision fatigue on low-energy days. The brain doesn't have to plan; it only has to choose.
- **Spirit:** In every tradition, people walked, gathered, or prayed in particular places. The place itself held memory, and stepping into it signaled a shift from chaos to sanctuary.

Reflection Prompt: My Sanctuary **Map** Write down:

- Three indoor places.
- Three outdoor places.
- One "micro-place" at home (even a window or a specific chair) that can be your anchor on days you can't go far. Post your map somewhere visible. When the critic says, "You have nowhere to go," your own handwriting will answer, "Here."

"A sanctuary is not about miles. It's about how your body feels when you arrive."

Reflection Prompt: Pick one of these five to practice for a week. Write down how the experience of that everyday task changed. Did you feel calmer, more awake, less rushed?

"Mindfulness doesn't need new time – it needs new attention."

5. The Emergency Drawer

Some days you won't remember your Happy List. The sky will be too grey, the critic too loud, the body too tired. On those days, don't think. Just open the drawer.

The **Emergency Drawer** is a small, physical reminder that you've prepared for this moment. It can sit in your desk at work, your bedside table, or even a small box on a shelf. The point isn't the container. The point is the message: *"You will forget. I will remember for you."*

What to Put Inside Fill it with small, sensory anchors that steady you fast such as:

- A square of dark chocolate.
- A postcard from a friend.
- A scented candle or a tiny bottle of essential oil.
- A playlist printed on paper with one uplifting song circled.
- A photo of a place where you felt calm.
- A handwritten note to yourself from a better day.

Why It Works

On heavy days, your thinking brain is tired. Decision-making feels impossible. Having a pre-made kit bypasses that fatigue and gives your nervous system instant cues of safety and care. Touch, scent, sight, and sound can all lower cortisol within minutes.

How to Use It

When you feel yourself sliding into overwhelm, don't wait until you "feel like" doing something. Open the drawer. Pick one item. Let it do its work — smell the oil, read the note, play the song, hold the photo. Stay with it for at least 60 seconds before moving on.

> **Reflection Prompt:** Start your Emergency Drawer this week. List three items you'll include right away, and one note you'll write to your future self.

"An emergency kit isn't indulgence.

It's proof you've left a light on for yourself."

Your Sacred Me-Time – The Quiet Joy That's Yours

Up to now we've been stocking your medicine cabinet with playlists, rituals, places and kits. But every winter medicine cabinet needs one more shelf: the space where you gather joys that belong only to you. Not the algorithm's list, not a friend's routine, not a highlight reel — **your own small acts of joy**.

This is the time that is *yours*. The hour no one schedules for you. The moment that does not need to be justified or judged. It might be early morning before the house stirs, or a lunch break with your phone on silent, or an evening pocket after the day has folded. The clock doesn't matter; what matters is that you claim a slice of it and treat it as sacred.

Think of it as your **"me-time altar"** or **"sacred me-time menu."** When you step into it, you're not escaping responsibility — you're fuelling it. A nervous system that's been given five, ten, or twenty minutes of true joy is steadier, kinder, and more creative in every other role you hold.

Here's how it can look:

- Painting for twenty minutes, even if the canvas stays unfinished.
- Sitting with a book of poetry and tea at sunrise.
- Walking a loop around your neighbourhood without headphones.
- Singing in the shower like it's a small concert.
- Taking a slow bath with eucalyptus oil after work.
- Gardening, knitting, sketching, writing a letter, playing an instrument, baking bread.

These aren't hobbies to "fit in" or photos to post. They're oxygen. They're how you remind your nervous system, *I am a whole person, not just a worker or caregiver.* They are a small act of sovereignty in a season that can otherwise feel like it's swallowing your time.

Reflection Prompt: My Unique Joy List
List 5-10 activities that lift you when you're alone. Mark the ones that make you feel the most joy. Pick one to do this week – morning, noon, or night – and notice how your energy shifts afterwards.

"Joy multiplies when it's shared – but it begins as a private well you draw from first."

Sharing Joy - Multiplying Your Light

Winter — both the season outside and the seasons of struggle inside — can shrink our worlds. Our homes feel smaller, our circles thinner. But joy multiplies when it's shared. A single spark you offer to someone else often glows brighter in you, too.

That doesn't mean curating a perfect, Instagram-worthy "Happy List" for others to admire. It means letting your real, personal joys spill into connection in ways that feel natural and human.

- **Swap playlists** with a friend who's also feeling the winter blues.
- **Host a comfort-watch evening** with one or two people instead of scrolling alone.
- **Start a "Happy Thread"** at work where teammates share small rituals that help them get through heavy days.

- **Invite a neighbour** for tea and toast instead of waiting for a formal dinner.

These aren't performances; they're invitations. They don't have to be polished, themed, or posted. They're simply your light meeting someone else's in the dark.

Why It Works

Shared joy releases oxytocin — the same bonding hormone that rises in firelit gatherings, shared meals, and old rituals. Even a quick text that says, "Here's a song that helped me this morning" tells your nervous system: *I'm not alone here.* And the act of giving reminds you of your own resourcefulness.

How to Use It

Pick one item from your Happy List and offer it to someone this week. A song, a show recommendation, a mug of soup. Let the act be small and genuine. No hashtags, no pressure, no performance. Just warmth.

> **Reflection Prompt:** Write down one simple way you could share an item from your Happy List with someone this week. How might that act shift both your day and theirs?

"Your Happy List is not a display case. It's a lantern. When you pass it on, the light doubles."

Closing Reflection - Firewood for the Soul

When the darkest days arrive — the snowstorm outside or the storm of self-doubt inside — you don't have to start from zero. You will already have stacked your firewood. Each song, each show, each small ritual on your Happy List is a log on that pile. Not a performance, not a borrowed list, but your own — chosen because it speaks to you, not because an algorithm or a magazine said it should.

This is what makes the Happy List powerful: it is yours. Built with intention, not imitation. Each item on it is a seed of calm, a spark of delight, a thread of belonging. When you use it, you are not escaping your winter; you are enriching it. You are proving to yourself, over and over, that even in the heaviest seasons you can create light.

So when the next dark day comes — and it will — you won't have to wonder what to do. You will open your "medicine cabinet" or what I love to call your "joy cabinet" and find joy waiting. A candle already set aside. A playlist ready to play. A sanctuary mapped. A small kindness prepared. Firewood for the soul.

Reflection Prompt: Look over your Happy List. Which item feels most alive to you right now? Which feels like a spark you could share with someone else this week?

"Happiness in winter isn't an accident. It's a practice of stacking small sparks until a fire grows."

CHAPTER NINE SUMMARY - THE HAPPY LIST: YOUR PERSONAL WINTER MEDICINE CABINET

Key Insight

After grounding yourself in acceptance, breath, gratitude, and self-kindness, this chapter invites you to grow branches of daily joy. It reframes self-care from a luxury into a sacred responsibility: tending to your own steadiness fuels every role you hold. The Happy List becomes your personal *winter medicine cabinet* – a collection of simple joys and micro-rituals that anchor you when energy runs low.

Core Metaphors

- Firewood Before the Storm - Every song, ritual, and comfort you gather becomes warmth to draw from on dark days.
- Medicine Cabinet - A shelf of sensory and emotional anchors chosen intentionally, not algorithmically.
- Fika / Kakkukahvi - Everyday pauses that turn coffee or tea into acts of presence – joy that tastes like light.

Practices for Everyday Joy

- Tiny Mindfulness Moments - Shower pauses, doorway breaths, first sips that steady the nervous system.
- Music as Medicine - Build a personal playlist as emotional grounding and gentle activation.
- Comfort-Watching as Anchoring - Familiar stories that calm through predictability and belonging.
- Joy Rituals That Warm the Day - Tea, candlelight, or cooking that reconnect you with sensory warmth.
- Places That Lift You (Sanctuary Map) - Spaces where your body exhales and your mind quiets.

- The Emergency Drawer - A small kit of comfort items and reminders for heavy days.
- Your Sacred Me-Time - Unscheduled, personal time reclaimed as self-nourishment.
- Sharing Joy - Passing your light forward through small, genuine gestures.

Reflection Prompts

- Which songs, shows, or rituals truly restore me?
- What spaces feel like sanctuary when days grow heavy?
- What three items would I place in my Emergency Drawer?
- How might I share one spark of joy with someone else this week?

Closing Meditation Mantra

"I stock my own firewood before the storm. I choose joy in small doses – music, warmth, presence – and let those sparks grow into steady light."

CHAPTER TEN

Carrying Your Calm: Bringing Inner Practices to Work and Beyond

There was a winter when my office calendar looked like a wall of bricks — back-to-back meetings stacked so tightly I felt no room to breathe. Literally. I'd walk in carrying the weight of a grey sky and sit at my desk already bracing for the day. By the third meeting I wasn't listening anymore — I was surviving. My chest tightened, my breath grew shallow, and I muted myself on calls just to catch air. Outwardly, I looked calm. Inwardly, I was battling panic.

If you've ever stared at a glowing screen with foggy eyes, felt your heart race during a meeting you didn't even want to be in, or ended a workday so drained you could barely stand — then you know what I'm talking about. Winter doesn't just shorten daylight; it shortens patience, focus and resilience.

I still remember the winter afternoon when, in the middle of presenting to senior executives, panic hit me like a wave. My throat tightened, my hands shook, and my voice cracked in ways I couldn't control. I mumbled an excuse and stepped out, heart pounding against my ribs. I sat down in the hallway, closed my eyes, and tried the simplest thing I could remember: inhale, hold, exhale. The first few breaths were jagged. The next few gave me just enough steadiness to walk back in and finish. It wasn't graceful. It wasn't impressive. But it was survival, and that mattered.

I've seen versions of that same storm in others. One friend, a lawyer, told me she'd sit in her car outside the courthouse on dark winter mornings, unable to make herself open the door. Another, a teacher, confessed she dreaded the last period of the day because she knew her patience would be gone before the bell. A founder once admitted his anxiety had nothing to do with investors or strategy — it was his calendar. The grid of meetings left him no space to breathe.

None of them needed a grand solution. What helped was something ordinary: three slow breaths before walking into the courtroom. A quiet pause before stepping back into the classroom. Five minutes blocked off between calls. Not cures, not magic — just enough of a crack in the storm for them to get through the next thing.

What I've learned is this: the practices we explored earlier — breath, gratitude, self-compassion — don't erase the panic, but they give it less power. They don't turn work into joy, but they can make it less unbearable. And sometimes, in the middle of a crowded day, that's already a kind of victory.

If panic can arrive in the middle of a presentation, it can also creep in quietly at the very start of the day. The truth is, workplace anxiety has a rhythm — mornings with their avalanches, afternoons with their fog, evenings that refuse to end. While winter sharpens the edges of fatigue and anxiety, these storms show up year-round, in every season, in every office.

This chapter is an experiment in real life. Up until now you've built your "Happy List," practised breath, affirmations, gratitude, self-compassion.

You've learned to steady yourself in winter, in loneliness, in small moments. Now we're going to mock up a day and see how those practices can travel with you — into a busy workplace, a home office, a commute, an evening. The goal isn't more to-dos; it's to show you how what you already know can become a living experience, a quiet companion walking beside you.

The Science: Why Winter Sharpens Workplace Anxiety

Before we step into the day itself, it helps to understand why work can feel heavier in winter (and at other high-pressure times of year). Earlier in this book we explored how the season reshapes our inner landscape: less daylight can mean lower serotonin, lingering melatonin, and nudged circadian rhythms. It isn't "just a mood" — biology and calendar collide.

- A large European study found employee productivity drops by nearly 20 percent in January compared to June, with shorter daylight hours and higher absenteeism named as key drivers.
- The American Psychological Association estimates seasonal stress and anxiety cost employers billions annually in lost output.
- In a Canadian workplace survey, almost half of employees reported that winter negatively affects their well-being, and nearly one in three noticed a direct decline in focus and performance.

This is the hidden storm inside organisations: not laziness, not lack of discipline, but a workforce whose biology is out of step with its calendar. Deadlines don't adjust to early sunsets. Budgets don't pause for melatonin dips. The clash shows up in real ways — missed decisions, slower thinking, fatigue during morning meetings, tension that flares faster.

And yet there's another truth: the practices you've been building — breath, gratitude, affirmations, self-compassion — aren't just personal rituals. They're workplace tools. They steady the nervous system between calls, widen perspective when the inbox feels like an avalanche, and remind you that productivity is not force, it's rhythm. Feeling less resilient in January doesn't mean you're weak — it means you're human. And being human means you also have access to practices that can restore flow, even in the storm. This chapter shows you how to carry those practices with you — into mornings, meetings, commutes, and the hours after work — so calm travels alongside you instead of staying behind on the meditation mat

Morning: Setting the Day's Weather

How you enter the morning sets the weather for everything that follows. Whether you're stepping into a commute, opening a laptop at home, or caring for others before your own tasks begin, the first hour plants the tone for the whole day. Winter makes this more visible, but the rhythm is year-round: mornings with their avalanches, afternoons with their fog, evenings that refuse to end.

There was a season when my own mornings were reaction first, breath later. The alarm would go off in darkness, I'd hit snooze, tumble straight from pillow to inbox and feel behind before the day even began. That single choice — to start in a rush — seeded anxiety that stayed with me all day.

Sleep researchers have a name for this: "sleep inertia." Fragmented, rushed waking leaves your mind groggy, your focus dulled and your stress threshold lower. Each snooze reinforces the sense of being late. Rising gently but firmly, once, gives your body a clear signal: a new day has begun.

When I finally began to practise what I teach, the shift was small but real. After my shower I let the warm water and slow breathing be my reset: three deep belly breaths, one short affirmation whispered into the steam. Before touching a screen, I opened the blinds and stood for a moment in the light. I chose one short sentence — "Light before inbox" — and carried it with me to my desk. Two minutes. That was it. It didn't make work easy, but it softened the storm before it started.

You might also revisit the "5 Tiny Mindfulness Practices for Mundane Moments" from the Happy List chapter; those little sparks are perfect for mornings like this. They're reminders that calm doesn't live only on the meditation mat — it can infuse ordinary acts like making tea, brushing teeth, or locking the door.

Here are three simple anchors many people find helpful to begin their day:

Three Morning Anchors

These small steps take less than two minutes but act as "mini bridges" from your morning routine into the working day. They're the way you carry your calm, rather than leave it behind.

1. Choose Inspiration Before Anxiety
Begin the day by deciding what sets your tone. Before opening your laptop or scrolling news and social feeds, choose something that lifts rather than drains — light, breath, a line from an affirmation, a quiet moment at the window. Even a single minute of "input you choose" before "input that chooses you" steadies the nervous system for what follows.

2. Three Breaths at the Threshold
Anxiety often spikes just before the day begins — walking into the building, logging onto Zoom, or opening the inbox. Before crossing that threshold, pause for three slow belly-deep breaths: inhale for four, exhale for six. This is enough to tell your body, "I am safe to begin." Use it at a red light on your commute, in the lobby before the elevator, or at your desk before you click "Join."

3. Gratitude + Affirmation + any signature meditation
Stress narrows perspective; gratitude widens it. Before you dive into tasks, write down one work-related gratitude and pair it with a short affirmation: "I'm grateful for ___, and today I choose to show up with ___."

Then, if you have a moment, close your eyes and visualise a warm sun rising inside your chest. With each inhale imagine light filling you; with each exhale imagine that light reaching into the day ahead. This simple visualisation connects gratitude, affirmation and breath, and starts your morning from a place of steadiness and hope.

> **Reflection Prompt:** Tomorrow morning, try one of these anchors before you open your inbox. Notice how the rest of the hour feels.

Midday: Navigating the Fog Hours

Even when a morning begins well, another challenge always arrives: the long middle stretch. In winter it takes the form of literal fog and fading light, but at any time of year afternoons can blur into exhaustion and doubt. Blood sugar dips, the sky darkens earlier, hours of sitting catch up with you. Many professionals describe this time as "the fog." It's not panic — it's a dull haze that makes simple things hard. Emails blur. Focus slips. You catch yourself rereading the same line again and again.

The fog convinces you that you're failing, when in reality it's biology and environment conspiring against you. Pushing harder rarely works. What does help is noticing when clarity has dimmed and placing a small reset there.

When I was first experimenting with carrying my practices into the workday, I noticed the biggest and deepest fog in the afternoon. If I reached for a snack or scrolled through my phone, the haze deepened. But if I paused for a drink of water, walked a few steps, or took three slow breaths at my desk, the day didn't magically become easy — but it stopped feeling impossible.

I also learned the power of a mindful lunch. One of my former bosses had a simple rule: when we sat down to eat, we talked about anything but work. No debriefs, no planning, no "quick questions" over sandwiches. Those thirty minutes of off-topic conversation — or even quiet — refreshed us more than an hour at our desks. Sometimes I'd simply eat without a screen or watch a short video I loved. Taking even a small break for lunch away from the storm breaks the cycle of depletion and gives the nervous system a reset.

Here are five tiny anchors many readers use in their own "fog hours":

Five Midday Anchors

1. **Fuel Check**
   Afternoon fog is often worsened by food choices — too much sugar, too little hydration. Before blaming yourself for fatigue, pause to check: Have I had water in the last hour? Did lunch leave me crashing? Keep a glass of water on your desk and a light snack (fruit, nuts) nearby.
2. **Mindful Lunch**
   Treat lunch as a true pause, not an extension of work. Step away from your screen. Talk about something other than work with a colleague. Watch or read something you love. Even fifteen minutes of "mental off time" can refresh you more than a working lunch.
3. **Task Swap**
   Fog makes high-focus work harder, but lighter or creative tasks can still flow. When your brain feels stuck, shift to something smaller: clearing a quick email, organising notes, brainstorming ideas. Save your most demanding work for higher-energy hours.
4. **Connection Reset**
   Human interaction refreshes the nervous system in ways solo effort cannot. Step into a colleague's office, send a quick "thank you" message, or call a friend for two minutes. The goal isn't a long chat — it's a brief reminder you're not alone in the fog.

5. **Joy Anchor**
   Small pleasures shift mood faster than forcing productivity. Keep one small joy within reach for the fog hour — tea you love, a short playlist, a photo, or even a stretch that feels good. Use it deliberately as a reset.

These aren't "hacks" to make you work harder. They're ways of giving your body and mind a crack of light in the middle of the day — a pause long enough for your nervous system to remember safety, clarity and choice.

> **Reflection Prompt:** What's your personal fog hour – 1 p.m., 3 p.m., just before school pickup? How could you create a mindful lunch or micro-reset there tomorrow?

Evening: Marking an Ending

And then comes the end of the day — which is rarely an end at all. Work has a way of following us into dinner tables, train rides, and sleepless nights. Winter darkness makes this more visible, but the struggle to draw a line between labour and rest is universal. Ending well is less about the clock and more about ritual — about telling both body and mind: "You are finished for now."

I've lived this too. There were evenings when I'd close my laptop but feel the meeting voices still circling in my head. I'd be sitting at my dinner table, replaying what I forgot to say, or scolding myself for mistakes I couldn't undo. The workday was technically over, but the critic was still at the table, whispering: "You didn't do enough. Tomorrow will be worse."

Many of my clients share the same experience. Some go straight from Zoom calls to cooking for a family, still mentally at work. Others finish late, then collapse into scrolling or snacking, feeling too wired to rest. Without a marker, your nervous system doesn't know the difference between "still working" and "done for today." Without kindness, the mind doesn't either.

When I began to experiment with closing rituals, I noticed my nights change. The practices didn't need to be big. A short walk after shutting the laptop. Writing down three completions from the day before I left the desk. Changing clothes or washing my face before dinner. These weren't chores; they were tiny signals: the day is over; you can let go now.

Here are five anchors you can use to mark your ending:

Five Evening Anchors

1. **The Completion List**
   The critic thrives on what's unfinished. Listing completions quiets its voice. Write down three things you completed — no matter how small — then add one task you'll leave for tomorrow. This is self-compassion in action: *Today is enough.*

2. **The Gratitude Close**
   Gratitude interrupts the critic's loop of blame and widens perspective. Note one thing at work you're grateful for — an act of kindness, a solved problem, a moment of calm. Speak it aloud if you can; gratitude softens the critic's edge.

3. **The Physical Signal**
   A repeated action tells body and mind: the workday is closed. Pair shutdown with a signal — changing clothes, washing your face, lighting a candle, or stepping outside briefly. This cue reminds both body and critic: we're finished here.

4. **The Transition Walk (or Stretch)**
   Movement metabolises stress that otherwise fuels the critic's story. Five to ten minutes of walking, or a slow stretch with breath, helps the body release what the mind keeps replaying.

5. **The Joy Carry-over**
   Choose one spark to carry home — a note of thanks, a small task you're proud of, or the memory of one calm moment. By naming it, you tell yourself: *this* is what I take forward, not the critic's story.

These anchors aren't about perfection. They're about giving yourself a gentle landing so you don't spill the noise of work into your evenings.

> **Reflection Prompt:** What's one small act that could signal "work is done" for you today? Write it down and try it tonight.

Weekends: Extending the Calm

All week long you've been practising small anchors — light before inbox, mindful lunches, three breaths at thresholds, gratitude notes, closing rituals at day's end. The weekend is where those practices have a chance to deepen. It isn't just time off from work; it's the soil where calm can take root.

If you've ever reached Saturday and felt too tired to enjoy it, or spent Sunday watching the clock until Monday returns, you're not alone. The same habits that make weekdays frantic can bleed into weekends: back-to-back plans, endless scrolling, trying to "catch up." The result is a weekend that blurs instead of restores.

You don't need a new set of tasks to fix this. You need a single anchor that turns pause into practice. Weekends are the best time to extend your daily meditation — not because you "should," but because the rhythm of the days finally gives you room. A ten-minute sit after your shower. A longer breath practice before breakfast. A gratitude note written slowly rather than rushed. These small expansions act like a slow recharge of the inner battery you've been using all week.

You can also:

- Plan one look-forward each day — a walk, a call, an hour with a book.
- Bring one weekday anchor into a weekend moment — three slow breaths before coffee, a gratitude note after a meal, opening the blinds before checking your phone.
- Create a gentle threshold between "week" and "weekend" — a short walk after logging off on Friday, changing clothes or lighting a candle to mark the shift.

These aren't chores. They're signals. They tell your mind and body: *we've arrived at the weekend; restoration is allowed.* Over time, the practices you've built for busy days stop feeling like things you "do" and start feeling like the way you live — even on Saturday morning, even on Sunday evening.

Reflection Prompt: What one anchor – especially meditation – could you carry into this weekend to make it restorative rather than rushed?

Rituals for Workdays (Flow, Not Force)

Portable, adaptable, human. Use what you already have.

1) No Back-to-Backs: Protect Space

Back-to-back meetings aren't just tiring; they're anxiety accelerants. Transitions regulate the nervous system – without them, stress compounds like interest. I once thought squeezing more in meant efficiency. It didn't. It meant panic. Now I defend pauses; even five minutes helps.

Base: Transitions settle the system.

Practice: In your five-minute buffer, close your eyes, one hand on chest/one on belly, inhale 4, exhale 6. Add a soft smile (it signals safety).
Where: Between Zooms at home, a hallway chair at the office, stepping away while travelling.
Reflection Prompt: Where can you protect a pause this week? Pick one meeting to surround with breathing space.

2) Mindful Pauses on day when you can't avoid Back to Back Meetings

Not every pause has to be profound.

- Inhale (belly rises)
- Hold 2
- Exhale (belly falls)
- Repeat ×3

Less than a minute – you'll return calmer and clearer.
Base: Belly breathing breaks fight-flight.
Practice: Three slow rounds whenever you shift tasks.
Where: Before unmuting, before another inbox dive, before entering a meeting room.

3) The Sunlight Sprint

When sun appears in winter, treat it as sacred. Even 2–5 minutes outside lifts mood and focus. Step out after a call, walk the block, or simply face the light and breathe.
(A client texted: "Two minutes in the sun – my brain exhaled.")
Base: Light supports mood and circadian rhythm.
Practice: 2–5 minutes of natural light.
Where: Office doorway, home balcony, airport curb.

4) The Two-Minute Desk Reset

When 2 p.m. fog hits:

- Sit tall, feet flat

- Inhale nose 4
- Hold 2
- Exhale mouth 6
- Repeat ×5

Two minutes. Boardroom, café, airplane – anywhere.

Base: Fog = system fatigue; breath resets attention.

Practice: Five 4-2-6 cycles. Or any breathing technique from earlier chapters.

Where: Desk, meeting room, car, plane seat.

5) Movement as Medicine

Anxiety feeds on stillness; a rigid body convinces the brain it's trapped. Micro-move to break the spell.

- Stand during calls
- Roll shoulders hourly
- Take stairs
- Stretch between emails

These aren't workouts; they're reminders: *I am alive, I am safe, I am present.*

Base: Movement metabolises stress and interrupts tension loops.

Practice: One micro-movement each hour.

Where: Office, home workspace, classroom, airports.

6) Gratitude at the Desk

Winter narrows attention to what's wrong; gratitude widens it back.

Each morning, jot one work-specific gratitude: a colleague's kindness, a warm mug, a small task done.

Base: Gratitude shifts attention toward possibility.

Practice: One short line daily.

Where: Notebook, sticky note, phone.

Carrying Calm Through Days and Weeks

In this chapter you've done more than walk through a single day. You've learned how to let your morning anchors travel into meetings, how to soften the fog hours of afternoon, how to mark an evening so work doesn't follow you home, and how to create small after-work rituals even if you live alone or work from home. You've also stepped back to see the *week* as a rhythm: heavy Mondays, midweek pile-ups, Friday fades, weekends as restoration rather than overflow.

None of these steps are about adding more to-dos. They're about letting the practices you already know — breath, gratitude, self-compassion, your Happy List — become part of your natural daily and weekly pattern. Calm stops being a "thing you do" and starts being the texture of how you move through time.

As you begin to live this way, something subtle happens. You don't just get through days and weeks; you start to notice which conditions strengthen you and which begin to drain you. You see which rituals really anchor you, which companions lift you, and which patterns quietly pull you back into old habits. This awareness is the quiet bridge to the next part of your journey.

Because even with good anchors, old winds can blow. Algorithms, office dynamics, certain people or thoughts can sneak in and re-seed habits you thought you'd left behind. The next chapter is about recognising those "watch-outs" — not with shame, but with self-compassion — and learning how to shed what no longer serves you so your new practices can take root.

You've built a rhythm of light through your days and weeks. Now you'll learn how to keep that light from being dimmed by old patterns.

CHAPTER TEN SUMMARY - CARRYING YOUR CALM: WORK AND BEYOND

Key Insight

Calm isn't a ritual you leave on the mat; it's a rhythm you carry through your day. Small anchors – breath, gratitude, self-compassion, and tiny pauses – turn crowded days and long seasons into something steady. The goal isn't more to-dos, but learning to let what you already know travel with you through mornings, meetings, commutes, evenings, and weekends.

Core Metaphors

- Setting the Day's Weather - How you begin shapes the atmosphere that follows.
- Crack in the Storm - Even sixty seconds of awareness can reopen choice.
- Thresholds - Tiny doors between tasks or rooms where breath resets your role.
- Portable Light - Calm becomes a lantern you carry from desk to commute to home.

Practices for Everyday Grounding

- Morning Anchors - Choose inspiration before anxiety; take three threshold breaths; pair gratitude with a simple affirmation: "I'm grateful for ___, and today I choose ___."
- Midday Anchors - Pause for mindful lunch, stretch or walk, hydrate, and reset with one joy anchor – a sip, a song, or a short breath.
- Evening Anchors - Mark endings with three completions, one gratitude, and a physical cue like washing your face or stepping outside.

- Weekend Extension - Lengthen your meditation gently and carry one weekday anchor into the weekend to keep the rhythm alive.

Reflection Prompts

- Which morning anchor helps you enter the day with calm?
- Where is your personal "fog hour," and what 60-second reset fits there?
- What simple act can mark your workday's ending today?
- How will you extend one weekday practice into the weekend?

Closing Meditation Mantra

"I carry my calm – breath by breath, threshold by threshold. I choose light before noise, presence before rush, and kindness before pressure – at work, at home, in every season."

PART III

Watchouts

CHAPTER ELEVEN

When Old Leaves Return

"Real healing is meeting yourself kindly each time you circle back – old habits aren't failure, they're invitations to gentleness."

Learning to Let Go Again and Again

A forest in January looks honest. Branches bare, bark darkened with rain, ground soft with brittle leaves. The air smells of damp earth and old wood. In autumn the trees let go once, but storms and wind keep shaking loose what clings. A tree does not scold itself for this. It does not call itself weak. It simply releases again.

We, meanwhile, live in a storm of calendars, algorithms, other people's moods, and our own inner winters. We shed habits, clear clutter, start fresh — and then the gusts return. A week of mindful mornings slips into snoozed alarms. A ritual of evening journaling turns back into scrolling in bed. Sometimes the gust is internal: exhaustion, self-doubt, a low-light day. Sometimes it's external: a harsh email, a careless remark from a colleague, a friend who mocks your new ritual. One breeze and the critic — inside or out — wakes up and whispers, "See? Nothing ever lasts." One harsh email, a careless remark from a colleague, a single off-hand comment from someone we love, and suddenly the critic inside us wakes up again: *"Hello! You're failing."*

But relapse is not failure. It's rhythm. It's biology. Under stress or low light, the nervous system can favor shortcuts; subcortical habit systems may shift into autopilot. Old loops re-activate without asking for permission. Add a gust of outside negativity and the pull doubles. This isn't proof you're weak; it's proof you're alive.

The work of this chapter isn't to shame you back into discipline or to make your habits become a performance for outside approval. It's to help your nervous system — and your heart — practise a kinder response: notice sooner, release quicker, return more gently. To understand that your practices are yours, not theirs. Not a show, not a scorecard, but quiet acts of self-tending.

Every time you circle back, you are rehearsing persistence, not perfection. You're strengthening the part of you that can hold steady even when the gusts arrive. That's what real healing looks like: meeting yourself kindly each time you arrive at the same bend in the path.

"Falling back is not the opposite of progress. Returning kindly – especially in the face of outside gusts – is progress."

The Shadow Side of the Happy List

In the last chapter you built your Happy List — songs, shows, rituals, places, small joys. Done with intention, it's a medicine chest for the soul. But like any medicine, the dose matters. Too little and it doesn't help. Too much and it becomes poison.

A comfort show that once steadied you can slip into an eight-hour binge that leaves you emptier. A ritual cup of cocoa can become nightly sugar dependence. Playlists meant to soothe can drown the silence you need to hear yourself. And even a single sharp comment from someone else — "You watch too much TV," "You're wasting time," "You're still doing that silly ritual?" — can flip the switch from nourishment to shame. The critic, whether internal or external, pounces: *"See? You're hiding again. You're weak."*

Pause here. Breathe. This is not weakness. It's wiring. Under stress or low light the brain defaults to autopilot, craving the easiest comfort it knows. A habit loop (rigger → urge → action → outcome) reactivates without asking for permission. Add a careless remark from someone you trust, and shame doubles the pull.

The point of the Happy List was never perfection. It was to stack firewood before the storm, so that when the day goes dark you have a spark ready. Some nights you will use that spark as a lantern. Other nights you may fall asleep beside it. That's not proof you're failing — it's a signal to pause and recalibrate. Ask yourself gently: *"Is this nourishing me or numbing me right now?"* That question alone is already a return to awareness.

And here's the added dimension: joy practices need a **pulse**, not a cage. They are meant to be lived, flexed, adjusted — not graded. You're allowed to experiment, to set a timer on your comfort show, to swap cocoa for a walk, to take a break from a ritual that's lost its warmth. Self-permission keeps your Happy List alive instead of rigid.

Reflection Prompt:

- Which of my Happy List items genuinely refill me?
- Which risk turning into avoidance?
- What physical or emotional signals tell me I've crossed the line (foggy mind, irritability, heaviness)?
- What tiny adjustment (timing, setting, dose) could keep this joy as nourishment?

"Joy becomes medicine when chosen; it becomes noise when unconscious. The difference is noticing."

Habits That Creep Back

Whenever life feels heavy — shorter days, a demanding job, a loss, or just a season of stress — old patterns have a way of resurfacing. You can be practicing new habits for weeks, feeling steady, and then one harsh email, one critical remark from a colleague, or one night of poor sleep pulls you straight back into scrolling, snacking, or spiralling.

This isn't proof of failure; it's how your nervous system is wired. Habits live in the basal ganglia — your brain's autopilot. When you're tired or under pressure, the part of your brain that makes conscious, wise choices goes dim, and the old loop takes over (cue → craving → response → reward). That's why someone can journal diligently for ten days and suddenly find themselves doom-scrolling until 2 a.m. or reaching for comfort food at midnight.

This is not a moral flaw. It's human nature. Our ancestors survived by defaulting to familiar behaviours under threat; your nervous system still does the same. The work isn't to become perfect. It's to become **persistent at good things** — to notice sooner, to pause sooner, and to return sooner. Every time you catch yourself mid-loop and take one conscious breath, you're already practising a new groove.

Think of it like walking a snowy path. Each time you take the kinder route, even for one step, you deepen that track. Over time the new path gets easier to find, even after a storm. This is what growth looks like in real life: not a flawless streak, but a shorter gap between drifting off and coming back.

Reflection Prompt:

- Which three habits return to me when my "inner winter" hits?
- What do they give me in the moment?
- What do they cost me over time?
- What gentle signal can I use to pause and choose again?

"Old habits aren't proof you've failed. They're proof you're human. Progress isn't perfection – it's shortening the distance between wandering and returning."

Returning Kindly

No tree scolds itself for the leaves it must drop again. It simply notices, lets go, and waits for new growth. That's the posture we're practising here.

Old patterns will creep back — not because you're weak, but because you're a human being in a noisy world. And that noise isn't only inside you. It lives in your environment: the culture of "always on," the meetings stacked without breaks, the constant scroll of other people's lives, the subtle pressure to be impressive even in your private rituals.

And when you're tired, that noise often takes its sharpest form: comparison. The critic doesn't just remind you of slips — it compares you with others who seem steadier, happier, more disciplined. But remember what you learned earlier: every time you measure your worth against someone else, you step away from your own path. Comparison isn't insight; it's distraction disguised as self-improvement. These external gusts can shake loose what you've just built just as easily as your own self-doubt.

I've felt those gusts too. Sometimes it's as small as a notification on LinkedIn — someone's promotion, an ex-colleague's new role, or a friend posting about another trip abroad to a destination I wanted to go. A moment earlier, I was grounded. Then, in a flicker, that calm shifts into a quiet ache: *am I moving fast enough? Doing enough? Being enough?* It's humbling to notice how quickly the mind can turn a celebration into self-critique.

When you return kindly, you quit that race. You stop running laps around other people's lives and start walking your own again — slower, steadier, more honest. Part of returning kindly is recognising those gusts for what they are. It's normal to drift. The work is simply to come back — again and again — not through judgment, but through awareness.

It's normal to want support or acknowledgement for the changes you're making. But if your practices depend on outside applause, every glance or scroll becomes a verdict. What you're building is yours, not theirs. Your breathwork, your rituals, your small joys aren't performances; they're quiet acts of self-tending.

So when you slip — whether because of your own critic or the noise around you — pause. Breathe. Remember: you're not failing; you're noticing. This is the practice. Use the tools you've built: put down the phone, step outside, take three slow breaths. Choose one nourishing thing. Begin again.

Real change isn't about never slipping. It's about shortening the distance between slipping and returning. Each gentle return is a rehearsal for growth. Persistence at good things — not perfection, not applause — is what slowly rewires your nervous system to expect kindness instead of criticism. And that clarity is what protects you from the validation trap: when your practices are for you, not for display, the noise of comparison loses its grip.

Reflection Prompt: Write your own "returning kindly" mantra. For example: "I noticed. I paused. I chose again. My worth is not erased by one mistake – or by someone else's opinion."

"Every gust – inside or out – is an invitation to hold your ground, return gently, and keep building what is yours."

Closing Section – The Return Ritual

You've now met the most persistent "old leaves," the habits that drift back, the tug of comparison, the sting of a careless comment. They're not evidence of weakness. They're evidence of being alive in a noisy world. Real healing isn't about never slipping; it's about noticing sooner, softening faster, and returning more kindly each time you do.

And that return begins the same way every time, trusting your chosen practices from the book.

1. Accept the moment. Whisper to yourself, "I slipped. That's human."
2. Breathe. One hand on your chest, one on your belly. Inhale for four counts, hold for two, exhale for six. Feel the knot loosen. Or your choice of the breathing exercises given earlier
3. Choose one gentle act. Step outside for a minute of air. Play a song from your Happy List. Open your Emergency Drawer.

This is not penance. It's practice. Every time you do it, you're rehearsing the book's central truth: that calm isn't a single breakthrough, it's a series of small, steady returns.

Your "Returning Kindly" Ritual

Create a small card or note for your desk, wallet, or phone background with these three lines:

- *I accept this moment without shame.*
- *I breathe, and my body remembers safety.*
- *I choose one nourishing thing and begin again.*

Whenever you notice an old leaf drifting back, read the card aloud or in your mind. Touch it if you can. This becomes your anchor — a ritualised version of everything you've learned so far.

Closing Reflection

Every page up to here has been a slow gathering of tools: acceptance, openness, food for body and mind, breath, affirmations, gratitude, self-kindness, happy lists. They are not trophies to display; they are choices you keep making.

When an old leaf drifts back or a comparison stings, your power is not in inventing something new but in returning to what you've already chosen. Pick one practice you built in the earlier chapters — a breath, a song, a gratitude line — and do it again, even if it feels small. **This path was never about staying ahead; it's about finding your way back, again and again.** That is how the architecture of calm becomes lived experience: not a single grand act, but hundreds of quiet re-choices that train your nervous system to meet life with steadiness and gentleness.

> *"Your rituals aren't there to impress the world;*
> *they're there to be chosen again and again –*
> *small doors back to yourself."*

CHAPTER ELEVEN SUMMARY - WHEN OLD LEAVES RETURN

Key Insight

Old habits drifting back aren't signs of failure; they're reminders that you're human in a noisy world. Real healing is the art of noticing sooner, softening faster, and returning more kindly. Each gentle return strengthens your inner steadiness and turns relapse into rhythm.

Core Metaphors

- Forest in January - Branches bare, leaves falling again and again; no scolding, only release.
- Gusts of Wind - Stress, fatigue, and stray remarks that shake your calm but can't uproot it.
- Snowy Path - Every kind return deepens the new track; the more you walk it, the easier it is to find.

Practices for Gentle Returning

- The Return Ritual - Accept: *"I slipped. That's human."* Breathe: one hand on chest, one on belly – inhale 4, hold 2, exhale 6. Choose: one nourishing act – a step outside, a song, or your Emergency Drawer.
- Joy Check - Ask, *"Is this nourishing me or numbing me?"* Adjust the dose, not the intent.
- Pause Mid-Loop - One conscious breath when an old habit surfaces is already a return.
- Guard Against Comparison - Remember your calm is personal, not performative. What's built for you doesn't need applause.

Reflection Prompts

- Which joys refill me, and which drift into avoidance?
- What habits reappear when my inner winter hits, and what do they cost over time?
- What gentle cue helps me pause and choose again?
- Write your own "returning kindly" mantra: *"I noticed. I paused. I chose again."*

Closing Meditation Mantra

"I return, not to fix what's broken, but to remember I was never broken at all."

CHAPTER TWELVE

Bloom in winter and shine in every season

Taking the Light Forward

Opening Note – A Hand on Your Shoulder

If Chapter 11 was about returning kindly when old leaves cling, this final chapter is about what you return *to*: a steadier centre you can carry into any season. We're not "finishing" the work so much as standing on a threshold together, turning to face life with the tools you've earned — acceptance, openness, breath, better words, real nourishment, humane rituals, and the courage to begin again.

All through this book you've been building a shelter. Every exercise you tried — the slow breath before a meeting, the gratitude line scribbled on a tired night — was another brick in a sanctuary you could return to when winter, outer or inner, felt too much. Breath steadied panic. Gratitude softened grey days. Rituals anchored you. A Happy List reminded you of warmth. You've been laying a hearth stone by stone, even on days you thought you were only surviving.

But shelter is not the destination. Shelter is what lets you heal so you can remember where you're going. This chapter is about moving from shelter to compass. The practices you've learned are not trophies or hacks; they're training. They're you laying a hand on your own shoulder and whispering, *I'm here. I'm safe. I know the way back.*

I want you to hear this as clearly on the last page as on the first: I'm with you in spirit. I wrote these chapters to sit beside you on heavy days and bright ones alike. If you ever want to share what's working, where you're stuck, or what you've discovered, you can reach me. Think of it as a lighthouse you can check in with while you navigate your own waters.

Winter — outer or inner — was our lens, not our limit. The point was never just to get through a season, but to practice a way of being you can bring to meetings, kitchens, quiet nights, and crossroads. What you've built here is portable: a light you can take with you.

Micro-Arrival Before We Begin

Place one hand on your chest, one on your belly. Inhale for four counts, hold for two, exhale for six. Whisper, "I carry the light. I carry it forward."

Reflection Prompt (60 seconds)

Take a breath. Feel the warmth of that small log you just named. Everything you've done in these chapters — every ritual, every breath, every kind word to yourself — has been about building a hearth inside you. Now we're going to open the door and step out with that hearth still glowing.

Winter was our teacher, but it was never meant to be a cage. The same steadiness you practised in darkness is the steadiness you'll carry into light.

The same breath you used to soften the critic in January can steady you in June. The same Happy List that warmed a long night can brighten a busy afternoon in August.

This chapter is where the book stops being a shelter and starts becoming a compass. You're not only someone who can return kindly when you slip; you're someone who can travel kindly when you grow. You're ready to move from "recovering" to "navigating" — bringing winter's wisdom into every season of your life.

Seasons as Teachers, You as Traveller

You've walked through winter in these pages, but winter was only the doorway. The real invitation has always been to learn the language of seasons — not as weather reports, but as metaphors for your own becoming.

Every culture that lives close to the land knows this: the year isn't a straight line, it's a spiral. Each loop brings you back to familiar places but with a new layer of understanding. In the same way, your inner life isn't just "problems to fix." It's a living cycle — beginnings, fullness, release, stillness.

- Spring shows you how to start again.
- Summer reminds you of abundance and expansion.
- Autumn rehearses letting go.
- Winter strips you back to essentials so you can see what remains.

Across cultures, this cycle was never just a calendar; it was a map for the soul.

- In Japan, the brief blaze of cherry blossoms each spring has long taught impermanence and return.
- Celtic peoples marked the Wheel of the Year with fire and harvest festivals, rehearsing beginnings and endings so no season felt like a surprise.

- Native North American tribes held winter councils where elders told stories to prepare the young for spring — wisdom stored like seeds.

These weren't random customs. They were ways of saying to each new generation: *the cycle you're living is ancient, and you're not the first to walk it.*

We've spent these chapters exploring winter because it's the hardest and the clearest. Without the bright noise of summer you can hear your own heartbeat. Without endless daylight you can see what really glows. But the point of learning winter is not to live there forever. It's to bring winter's wisdom into every season.

When you've practised steadiness in the dark, you carry that steadiness into the light. When you've learned to breathe and speak kindly to yourself when everything feels bare, you don't lose it when life blooms again — you deepen it.

Think of yourself now not as a tree caught in one season, but as a traveller who's learned to navigate all of them. You know how to rest when you must, shed what you can't carry, pick up a practice, open your heart again. That is the skill. That is the ancient wisdom.

Reflection Prompt: All these cycles point to something larger than seasons: direction. Every culture that marked the turning of the year also looked to the sky for orientation – a fixed star, a rising sun, a constellation. In the same way, the practices you've built are more than rituals to "get through" winter; they're your training for navigation.
When you know how to steady yourself in the dark, you begin to notice the small glimmers of light that tell you where you're headed. Those glimmers – a moment of joy, a flicker of curiosity, a sense of quiet rightness – are your North Star. It won't guide your every step, but it will guide you through every season.

Finding Your North Star in Every Season

When sailors of old crossed dark oceans, they didn't need a full map; they needed one fixed light. The North Star gave them orientation, not a step-by-step itinerary. In the same way, the practices you've gathered in this book are not just "winter survival tools." They're your training for navigation.

You won't always have perfect clarity about where life is taking you. Seasons shift, circumstances change, your inner weather moves from bright to overcast. But once you've learned to steady yourself — to breathe, to choose a ritual, to speak kindly when the critic appears — you've built an inner compass. And as the noise quiets, small glimmers start to appear: a moment of joy, a flicker of curiosity, a sense of quiet rightness. Those glimmers are your North Star.

Your North Star is not a five-year plan or a productivity hack. It's a felt sense of alignment: *this is who I am when I'm not bracing.* You don't have to name it perfectly. You only have to start noticing what glimmers — the activities, people, or places that make your body exhale and your heart lift — and let them guide your next small step.

Fluctuation isn't failure; it's proof of life. A heartbeat only works because it rises and falls. Breath only works because it comes and goes. Day becomes night; tides come in and out. Without dark, you'd never see the stars. Without silence, no music. Without pauses, no rhythm.

This is why we spent so much time with winter: not to live there forever, but to teach you how to be steady inside fluctuation — to enjoy each season, not because it's easy but because it's part of the dance. When you can greet winter with steadiness, spring with openness, summer with gratitude, and autumn with grace, you're not just surviving cycles — you're living them with orientation.

Start simple. Look back over these chapters. Which practice felt most like "me"? Which one surprised you with its joy? Which one gave you a glimpse of who you want to become? Those are clues to your North Star. Follow them gently. Let them orient you without forcing you.

Reflection Prompt: Write down three moments from the last few weeks of reading this book that felt like a "spark" – a hint of what lights you up, even briefly. How might you take one small step toward that spark in the next season?

"Your North Star isn't a destination.
It's the quiet rightness you notice when you steady yourself and look up."

When you learn to trust your North Star, you realise it was never just in the sky — it's been rising within you all along. That's the northern light within — your steady inner glow, guiding you through every season.

Carrying the Light Forward

You've spent these pages learning how to steady yourself when the winds rise, how to shed what no longer serves you, how to feed body and mind, how to breathe light back into dark hours. But the deepest lesson isn't about winter at all. It's about remembering that every season is a teacher, and that you carry its wisdom with you.

Winter showed you stillness and preparation. Spring will show you renewal. Summer will show you joy and fullness. Autumn will show you surrender. Without fluctuation there is no life; a flat line means not stability, but death. To live is to rise and fall, to warm and cool, to bloom and bare.

This rhythm is older than any calendar. In the Vedas and the Upanishads the soul is described as a traveller — eternal, unborn, and undying —

moving through countless cycles of experience (samsara) until it ripens into freedom. Each life, each season, each return is not a step backward but part of a greater spiral of learning. What you call "slipping" or "starting over" is, from that wider view, the soul rehearsing its own liberation: shedding what is no longer needed, testing new ground, returning more awake each time.

That is why the practices you've gathered here aren't trophies or hacks. They're your portable hearth, your handrail on the spiral. They are how you keep walking the path of return. When you slip — and you will — come back to the breath, the small ritual, the kind sentence. Each gentle return is a micro-initiation, training your nervous system to expect kindness instead of criticism and your soul to remember its own brilliance.

Somewhere in those small glimmers — one breath, one walk, one reframed word — you'll notice something larger: a direction beginning to glow. It won't arrive as a five-year plan. It will arrive as a quiet rightness: *this feels like me.* In the Vedic view this is your dharma, your inner alignment, your North Star. Follow it in small steps. Let it guide you out of winter into a life that feels aligned, not just endured.

I wrote this book not as an expert talking down, but as a **companion walking beside you**. On every heavy morning and every hopeful night, I want it to feel like a hand on your shoulder whispering, *"You're not alone. You're practising."* Some of the meditations from the book are also available on my website, www.thecalmmind.co. And if you ever want to share what's working for you, where you feel stuck, or what you're discovering, you can reach me anytime at **connect@thecalmmind.co**. Think of it as a lighthouse you can check in with while you navigate your own waters.

This is the last page, but not the end. It's the moment where shelter becomes compass, where surviving becomes creating, where the northern light within you stops being a metaphor and starts being your way of seeing.

Close your eyes. Place one hand on your heart, one on your belly. Inhale slowly, exhale gently, and whisper:

I carry a light that is mine alone — and I choose to keep it moving forward.

Then open your eyes. Step into your next season.

CHAPTER 12 SUMMARY - BLOOM IN WINTER AND SHINE IN EVERY SEASON

Taking the Light Forward

Key Insight

The practices you've built are not trophies or hacks; they're your portable hearth. Each breath, ritual and kind sentence is a handrail on a spiral path, helping you return to yourself and carry steadiness into every season. In Vedic thought the soul travels through endless cycles, learning and refining until it awakens. Every small return you make is part of that timeless journey.

Core Metaphors

- *Portable Hearth*: what you've built isn't a single shelter but a light you can take anywhere.
- *Spiral Path*: like the soul in the Vedas, you circle back not to repeat, but to deepen.
- *North Star / Dharma*: your quiet inner rightness, glimmering through practices, guiding next steps.

Practices for Carrying the Light Forward

- Micro-Arrival - Place one hand on your chest, one on your belly. Inhale for four, hold for two, exhale for six. Whisper, "I carry the light. I carry it forward."
- Return to One Practice - Pick one tool from this book (breath, meditation, gratitude, affirmation, song). Do it again, even if it feels small. Each choice is a log on the fire you'll carry into the rest of your life.
- Notice Glimmers - Keep a simple list of moments of quiet rightness. These are clues to your North Star.

Reflection Prompt

Which practice from this book feels most yours right now? Which small step could bring that light into the next season?

Closing Meditation Mantra

"I am walking a timeless path. Each return is progress. I carry the light forward."

"Carry the Light"

You came to these pages in winter —
hands cold, breath thin,
looking for a small flame.
You leave with a hearth in your chest.

Every practice you chose,
every kind word you whispered,
stacked its own log on the fire.

Old winds may rise again.
Old leaves may drift back.
But you have learned the quiet art of returning —
breathing once,
softening once,
choosing once more.

So walk out into your next season.
Let your breath be your compass,
your small joys be your lantern,
and your gentleness be the proof
that you are already whole.

And if ever the nights feel long,
look north —
not to the sky, but within.
The same light that dances across frozen horizons
now lives quietly in you.
It is your northern light —
a calm that guides, even through the darkest hours.

Remember:
this light is yours.

It was here all along.
Now it travels with you.

I carry the light.
I carry it forward.

EPILOGUE

Living the Light

The northern lights are not always visible. Sometimes clouds veil them, sometimes the sun outshines them — yet they are never gone. The same is true of the light within you. Calm does not mean the absence of storms; it means remembering your compass when the wind returns.

The practices you've met in these pages — breath, reflection, stillness, and self-kindness — are not tasks to perfect, they are pathways to return. They help you realign when life pulls you off course and the clouds of thoughts emerge. Each time you breathe through a hard moment, listen without reacting, or choose gentleness when you could choose blame, you are carrying the northern light forward.

You won't always feel radiant. Some days will dim; others will flare. That is the rhythm of being human. But even in those darker hours, trust this: the light does not vanish; it waits. One breath, one kind thought, one act of courage, and it stirs again.

The light within you was never something to find. It was something to remember. Now that you've remembered — live it.

For Additional Book resources please visit - www.thenorthernlightwithin.com

Or write to connect@thecalmmind.co

About the Author

Calmness. Purpose. Joy.

These three qualities run through everything Ashish Singh creates. A multi-award-winning life and wellness coach and founder of The Calm Mind—featured on top-coach lists in Toronto, Canada— he has spent more than 15 years guiding clients through stress, burnout, relationship shifts, and major life transitions. His approach blends Eastern-inspired mindfulness and energy practices with Western behavioural science to offer practical, evidence-based ways of finding steadiness and light in every season of life.

Having travelled to more than twenty-two countries across four continents, Ashish draws inspiration from the diverse cultures, landscapes, and spiritual traditions he has encountered. These journeys have deepened his understanding of what it means to find calm and connection—whether in a bustling city, a quiet mountain village, or the frozen silence of the poles.

Before becoming a full-time coach, Ashish spent 18 years leading teams and shaping brands in his corporate life—experience that grounds his coaching in real-world pressures and change rather than theory alone. The practices in *The Northern Light Within* were tested first in his own life, then refined through years of guiding others.

Clients describe him as "a guiding light" and "someone who can hold your hand and lead you toward peace." They come for clarity, leave with steady habits, and often stay for the quiet companionship of a coach who has walked the path himself.

Today, Ashish continues to write and coach not from a distance, but as a companion—someone who knows what it is to sit in the dark and still reach for light. Through The Calm Mind, he offers one-to-one sessions, group programmes, and speaking engagements designed to help people find calm, clarity, and purpose—wherever they are in their journey.

Learn more or reach out at

www.thecalmmind.co.

Coaching and content offered by The Calm Mind are intended for personal growth and are not substitutes for therapy or medical care.

Notes & Sources

The Northern Light Within integrates established research from psychology, neuroscience, and contemplative traditions. Readers are encouraged to explore the following key sources for deeper study.

Mind–Body Connection & Breathwork

Benson, Herbert. *The Relaxation Response.* HarperTorch, 1975.

Porges, Stephen W. *The Polyvagal Theory: Neurophysiological Foundations of Emotions, Attachment, Communication, and Self-Regulation.* W. W. Norton & Company, 2011.

Brown, Richard P., and Patricia L. Gerbarg. "Sudarshan Kriya Yogic Breathing in the Treatment of Stress, Anxiety, and Depression." *Journal of Alternative and Complementary Medicine* 11, no. 4 (2005): 711–717.

Feldman, Gary, et al. "Mindfulness-Based Stress Reduction and the Relaxation Response." *Psychosomatic Medicine*(2010).

Nutrition, Mood & the Gut–Brain Axis

Jacka, Felice N., et al. "A Randomized Controlled Trial of Dietary Improvement for Adults with Major Depression (The SMILES Trial)." *BMC Medicine* 15, no. 23 (2017).

Dash, S., Clarke, G., Berk, M., and Jacka, F. N. "The Gut Microbiome and Diet in Psychiatry: Focus on Depression." *Current Opinion in Psychiatry* 28, no. 1 (2015): 1–6.

Neuroplasticity & Emotional Regulation

Davidson, Richard J., and Sharon Begley. *The Emotional Life of Your Brain.* Penguin, 2012.

Doidge, Norman. *The Brain That Changes Itself.* Penguin, 2007.

Neff, Kristin D., and Christopher Germer. *The Mindful Self-Compassion Workbook.* Guilford Press, 2018.

Neff, Kristin D. "Self-Compassion, Self-Esteem, and Well-Being." *Social and Personality Psychology Compass* 5, no. 1 (2011): 1–12.

Self-Compassion, Gratitude & Positive Psychology

Emmons, Robert A., and Michael E. McCullough. "Counting Blessings Versus Burdens: An Experimental Investigation of Gratitude and Subjective Well-Being in Daily Life." *Journal of Personality and Social Psychology* 84, no. 2 (2003): 377–389.

Seligman, Martin E. P. *Flourish: A Visionary New Understanding of Happiness and Well-Being.* Free Press, 2011.

Fredrickson, Barbara L. *Positivity.* Crown Archetype, 2009.

Loneliness, Connection & Boundaries

Cacioppo, John T., and William Patrick. *Loneliness: Human Nature and the Need for Social Connection.* W. W. Norton & Company, 2008.

Brown, Brené. *The Gifts of Imperfection.* Hazelden, 2010.

Linehan, Marsha M. *Cognitive-Behavioral Treatment of Borderline Personality Disorder.* Guilford Press, 1993 — foundational for compassionate boundary work and dialectical balance.

Stress, Resilience & Seasonal Change

Rosenthal, Norman E. *Winter Blues: Everything You Need to Know to Beat Seasonal Affective Disorder.* Guilford Press, 2021 (4th ed.).

Kabat-Zinn, Jon. *Wherever You Go, There You Are: Mindfulness Meditation in Everyday Life.* Hyperion, 1994.

Sapolsky, Robert M. *Why Zebras Don't Get Ulcers.* Holt Paperbacks, 2004.

Spiritual & Philosophical Roots

The Bhagavad Gita.

The Dhammapada.

Rumi, Jalaluddin. *The Essential Rumi.* Trans. Coleman Barks. HarperOne, 1995.

Hafez. *The Subject Tonight Is Love.* Trans. Daniel Ladinsky. Penguin, 1996.

Upanishads, various translations — referenced for cyclical philosophy and the soul as traveller (*samsara*).

Easwaran, Eknath. *Essence of the Upanishads: A Key to Indian Spiritual Thought.* Nilgiri Press, 2007.

Music, Ritual & Sensory Anchors

Chanda, Mona L., and Daniel J. Levitin. "The Neurochemistry of Music." *Trends in Cognitive Sciences* 17, no. 4 (2013): 179–193.

Feldman Barrett, Lisa. *How Emotions Are Made: The Secret Life of the Brain.* Houghton Mifflin Harcourt, 2017.

Stern, Daniel N. *The Present Moment in Psychotherapy and Everyday Life.* W. W. Norton & Company, 2004.

Cultural & Seasonal Practices

Löfgren, Orvar, and Jonas Frykman. *Culture Builders: A Historical Anthropology of Middle-Class Life.* Rutgers University Press, 1987 — contextual background on *fika* and Scandinavian seasonal culture.

Honkasalo, Marja-Liisa. "Kakkukahvi: Ritual, Hospitality, and Everyday Care." *Ethnologia Europaea* (2016).

Nelson, Melissa K., and Danielle Endres (eds.). *Indigenous Ecologies and the Seasons of the Earth.* University of Arizona Press, 2022 — for cyclical worldviews referenced in the "Seasons as Teachers" section.

General Inspirations

Frankl, Viktor E. *Man's Search for Meaning.* Beacon Press, 2006.

Thich Nhat Hanh. *Peace Is Every Step.* Bantam, 1992.

Chopra, Deepak. *The Healing Self.* Harmony, 2018.

David, Susan. *Emotional Agility.* Avery, 2016 — for adaptive self-regulation and returning kindly.

Siegel, Daniel J. *Aware: The Science and Practice of Presence.* TarcherPerigee, 2018.

Closing Note

The *North Star* and *Northern Light Within* metaphors draw from universal navigation imagery found across Indigenous, maritime, and Vedic traditions. They are used here as symbolic representations of inner guidance and alignment, not as religious or scientific claims.

Important Information & Copyright

This book is intended for informational and inspirational purposes only. It reflects the author's personal experiences, reflections, and practices that have supported well-being for himself and his clients.

It is not intended to diagnose, treat, cure, or replace professional medical, psychological, or therapeutic advice, diagnosis, or treatment. Readers are strongly encouraged to consult qualified healthcare professionals before beginning any new breathing, meditation, or lifestyle practice—particularly if they have pre-existing health conditions, are pregnant, or are under medical supervision.

Every effort has been made to ensure the accuracy and integrity of the information presented. However, the author makes no warranties or representations of any kind, express or implied, regarding the completeness, reliability, or suitability of the content, and expressly disclaims all liability for any loss, injury, or adverse outcome arising directly or indirectly from the use or application of the material in this book.

By reading this book, you acknowledge and agree that you are voluntarily engaging in any practice at your own discretion and risk, and accept full responsibility for your personal health, safety, and well-being. Approach each practice gently, with self-awareness and care.

This work has been created with the sole intention of promoting greater calm, clarity, and kindness in everyday life. Trust your own pace, listen to your body, and return to your breath whenever you need to.

Published by: Ashish Singh
Toronto, Canada
www.thecalmmind.co
Published in Canada / Distributed Worldwide
ISBN: 978-1-0698609-0-3

Made in United States
Cleveland, OH
17 June 2026